ORIGINAL
MUSTANG
1967–1970

Other titles available in the *Original* series are:

ORIGINAL
MUSTANG
1967–1970

by Colin Date

MOTORBOOKS

First published in 2006 by Motorbooks, an imprint of MBI Publishing Company, Galtier Plaza, Suite 200, 380 Jackson Street, St. Paul, MN 55101-3885 USA

The information in this book is true and complete to the best of our knowledge. All recommendations are made without any guarantee on the part of the author or Publisher, who also disclaim any liability incurred in connection with the use of this data or specific details.

This publication has not been prepared, approved, or licensed by Ford.

We recognize, further, that some words, model names, and designations mentioned herein are the property of the trademark holder. We use them for identification purposes only. This is not an official publication.

MBI Publishing Company titles are also available at discounts in bulk quantity for industrial or sales-promotional use. For details write to Special Sales Manager at MBI Publishing Company, Galtier Plaza, Suite 200, 380 Jackson Street, St. Paul, MN 55101-3885 USA

Library of Congress Cataloging-in-Publication Data

Date, Colin, 1956-
    Original Mustang, 1967-1970 / Colin Date.
       p. cm.
    Includes index.
    ISBN-13: 978-0-7603-2102-7
    ISBN-10: 0-7603-2102-7
 1. Mustang automobile—History. I. Title.
    TL215.M8D382 2002
    629.222'2—dc22

                                    2006007711

Editor: Amy Glaser
Designer: Chris Fayers

Printed in China

On the cover: A 1969 Mach 1 in Candy Apple Red. Although they look factory correct, the chin spoiler and rear window Sports Slats are aftermarket accessories. (Neither were available on the Mach 1 for 1969.) Over the years, they have become a popular addition to many Mustangs.

On the frontispiece: Like the 1967 models, 1968 Mustangs featured Mustang script lettering and the tri-shield emblem with engine callouts on the lower fenders. The engine designator was for V-8-powered cars only.

On the title pages: The Mustang GT fastback for 1967 poses at the Columbia River Gorge.

On the back cover: The Texas license plate says it all. This is the Trans-Am-inspired Boss 302 for 1969 in Bright Yellow.

On the contents page: The iconic '67 Shelby GT350 in Raven Black.

Contents

Acknowledgments

I'd like to offer my sincere thanks to a number of folks who helped bring this book to fruition.

For their expertise in all things Ford and their seemingly endless patience with me, thanks go out to Dick Rozum, John Rotella, and Bill Atol. These three gentlemen offered up their valuable time, energy, and resources to help me complete this book.

To my good friend and colleague Tom Shaw, who let me use several "hard to get" photographs from his vast collection of 1967–1970 Mustang and Shelby photography.

To "Fast" Eddie Stokes (fehotrodshop@aol.com), Joyce Donaldson (www.photosbyjoyce.net; joyce@photobyjoyce.net), and Doug Bennett (www.dougbennettphotography.com; doug@dougbennettphotography.com) for their wonderful lens work on much of the Shelby sections.

To Bryan Lowry, for coordinating the Colorado-based photographers named above.

To Marlon Mitchell, president and founder of the All-Mustang and Ford Club of Southern California for putting me in contact with all the folks who offered their valuable time and their incredible Mustangs for photography: Mike Vernarde, Dennis Piper, Bob Wells, Joe Rupp, Shirley Mac-Cartney, Jeff Spencer, Larry Vigus, Pat Figini, Ross Childers, and Brian Childers.

To my editors, Peter Bodensteiner and Amy Glaser. Amy came on midstream through this project and helped me through my looming deadline.

To my daughter Kim, who helped me more than she will ever know.

To my good Lord, who has always guided me every step of the way.

Introduction

What goes through your mind when you think of the late 1960s Mustang? Country club cruiser, boulevard bruiser, or a bit of both? I'll bet Frank Bullitt's Highland Green 1968 fastback comes to mind! I remember when the Mustang changed completely for the 1967 model year. Up until then, even at the tender age of 10, I remember the first generation Mustangs (1965–1967) captivating Toronto, the city I lived in. They were brand-new-on-the-scene pony cars, and it seemed the whole world was in awe of them.

Then came 1967, and everything changed again. The new Mustangs were more serious looking in my young mind. I remember seeing them advertised on television and in the newspapers, but I hadn't seen one in person until my dad got a phone call from one of his buddies who said that he and his wife had just bought a brand new 1967 Mustang convertible. It was Springtime Yellow with a black interior and black convertible top. I just about flipped out! (Don't forget it was the 1960s and "flipping out" was the thing to do back then.) I had to go see this car.

My dad was never a big car guy, so I don't think he realized the urgency of the situation. I needed to see that car right now! A few days later when I finally got to lay eyes on it, I wasn't disappointed. The convertible was beautiful to say the least, but being a ragtop and yellow, it seemed like more of a "girl's" car to me at the time. (Sorry) A short while later, I saw a Raven Black fastback with styled steel wheels and a black interior. That did it for me! I don't remember what engine it had, but at that point I didn't care. That 2+2 was the toughest looking thing I'd ever seen.

All the 1967–1970 Mustangs came in three body styles: hardtop, fastback (later called SportsRoof), and convertible. It's amazing how each body changed the car's personality so much. Hardtops always looked responsible, like the owner was just carefree and spirited enough to have purchased a Mustang, but that was about it. Chances are, and I'm generalizing here, the car was a six-banger. Typically, the hardtop drivers wanted that sporty look and feel, but weren't exactly speed demons. Fuel economy and general thriftiness seemed to typify this demographic.

Convertibles were for the glam set. The folks who bought ragtops were ready for adventure and open-highway cruising. They were the kind of people who didn't care about luggage capacity or fuel economy. These cars always seemed to have V-8 engines, but usually the smaller displacement versions. A GT convertible was about the epitome of glam, and a big-block car meant you were one serious cruiser. The fastback, on the other hand, was to me what Mustangs were all about. Make it a 390 or a 428, drop in a toploader, and you've got yourself what a Mustang should be! Aggressive good looks, tire-smoking drag strip performance, and style to spare. That's my take on America's first pony car, but given the Mustang's overwhelming popularity, I'm sure there are millions out there who have their own take on Ford's most successful car ever.

I wrote *Original Mustang 1964½–1966* for MBI Publishing Company back in 2002. It was my first book and it was one tough assignment, but I had a blast writing and shooting the photos for the book. I learned a lot about those cars and managed to jog many memories back into this thick ol' skull of mine. This book, *Original Mustang 1967–1970* is a follow-up piece, and to tell you the truth, it was a lot tougher to put together. The 1965–1966 Mustangs were all very similar without a lot of change happening over the 2½ years of production. There were only a few different trim groups, and the changes were pretty much kept to a minimum.

The 1967–1970 Mustangs were a whole different ball game. The 1967 models started out mellow enough and seemed like an easy continuation of the 1966 model, huge changes notwithstanding. There were still three basic cars, and the engines were the same except for the 390, and the king of the heap was the GT. After that chapter, however, things became much more complicated. The year 1968 introduced more trim groups, options, and engines.

After that, 1969 and 1970 expanded even more. Sports Roofs were now the big deal. Mach 1s and Grandés were part of the action and Boss 302s and 429s came out of the woodwork. Decor groups and colors galore. Wheel styles, interior trim, body striping, and specialty models as far as the eye could see! In 1969, there were 10 available engines. Beginning to see the picture? Mustangs became a lot more complicated, but in my humble opinion, they only became better. Power, comfort, convenience, and good looks all came together to finesse what was already America's favorite pony car.

Throughout the 1960s, Ford had some competition with Chevy's Camaro, Pontiac's Firebird, and Mopar's E-body cars (Barracuda and Challenger), but the competition was nothing Ford couldn't handle. Camaro came closest in 1970, when it was within 66,633 units of Mustang, but by then pony cars and muscle cars were on the way out. Mustang ruled then, as it does now.

There are many books on Mustangs out there. Most of them tend to cover all years and seem to water down the facts and figures. Years and options are glossed over with no real attention to charting the changes. This book attempts to offer you a more concise picture with *Original Mustang 1967–1970*. I hope it provides valuable reference material for you, and it'll probably look great on your coffee table, too.

Blessings to you,
Colin Date

Chapter 1

1967–1970 Mustang Primer

A lot has been said about Mustang's major facelift as it became a late 1960s pony car. From its intro midyear in 1964 as a 1965 model and through the 1966 model year, America's sweetheart was a stylish compact, and it offered plenty of glam for the suburban set. It was the car to be seen in and was part a whole new category of vehicle: the pony car.

In the Mustang's early years, it held the country's attention and had little or no competition. Sales thrived with almost 1.3 million cars being produced! General Motors and Chrysler appeared to be asleep at the switch, but of course, they weren't. Camaros, Firebirds, and Barracudas were lurking in the shadows. In 1967 Ford's "shootin' fish in a barrel" days were over, which didn't come as a shock to the Blue Oval boys. You can't expect to capture 100 percent of the market all of the time. After all, there were Chevy and Mopar guys out there who were waiting for something to come along that would blow the Mustangs into the weeds. But Ford had plans to take its beloved sporty

ABOVE: The king of them all was this 1969 Boss 429 in Wimbledon White shown here against the Colorado Rockies. BELOW: The 1967 and 1968 Mustangs featured "Mustang" lettering on early 1967 cars and "Mustang" script with the tri-shield logo. On eight-cylinder cars, the ci displacement was featured on the logo.

The pop-open gas cap was an option for 1968.

The 1970 Mustangs went back to the two-headlight configuration, and the running horse emblem was back in the middle of the grille. Simulated air scoops resided where the 1969 version placed its headlights.

The 1967 taillights continued on in the traditional Mustang three-bar design. The look carried on over into the 1968 model year.

compact to the next level just in time to face the now ravenous competition.

The year 1967 was a big turning point year for Mustang. The original pony car was still shattering sales records (although 1967 sales were decidedly less than the previous year: 472,209 versus 607,568 in 1966), and still was the measure by which all others were judged. But with the advent of General Motors' (GM) new Camaro (and to lesser extents, the Pontiac Firebird and Plymouth Barracuda), Ford decided to ramp up Mustang's styling, size, and firepower. As the 1960s progressed, style and power became more and more important. GM's F-body cars started out subdued enough, but they quickly transformed with more aggressive styling and under-the-hood grunt. In 1967, the Barracuda became less of a Valiant and more of a Road Runner. Big-block performance was now the word of the day.

As the competition turned up the burners on the style and power fronts, so did Ford. Increases in length, width, and engine displacement took place in 1967. The 1967 and 1968 Mustangs were sleeker versions of their forebears, and for the first time in Mustang history, big-block motors were offered. The years 1969 and 1970 saw another facelift and, you guessed it, more power.

The result was Ford's darling of the country club set was transformed into a bona fide muscle car, and Camaro owners now had something to worry about. Mid- to upper-14-second quarters in the high 90s were easily attainable right out of the box.

Standard gas cap for 1968.

The top-of-the-food-chain 428 Super Cobra Jet with Ram Air.

Notice anything unusual underneath this base Mustang hardtop? The staggered shocks give it away. This is a 428 Cobra Jet–equipped car. Note the primer showing through the body paint.

ABOVE: The air cleaner lid on the Boss 302s was chromed with a Boss 302 engine callout. BELOW: The 1969 Boss 302 came with a 780-cfm Holley four-barrel carburetor.

The mighty Cobra Jet Shaker scoop jutted out of the hood and literally shook when the engine was accelerated.

Production

The 1967–1970 Mustangs were manufactured by Ford Motor Company in three assembly plants in the United States: Dearborn, Michigan; Metuchen, New Jersey; and San Jose, California. The cars came in three different body styles and all were two-door models: hardtop, 2+2 fastback, and convertible. Cars from each of the production facilities were designated with a district sales office (DSO) code to indicate which area of the country they would be sold.

The numbers don't lie. A total of 1,280,190 Mustangs were built between 1967 and 1970. Compare that number to the 1,288,557 Mustangs that sold during the first two model years of life. A number of reasons led to 8,367 fewer cars being built over the later four-year period. The 1965 and 1966 cars started a brand new segment in the

1967 FORD MUSTANG PRODUCTION FIGURES

63A fastback standard (bucket seat)	53,672
63B fastback Decor Group (bucket seat)	17,389
63C fastback standard (bench seat)	1
65A hardtop standard (bucket seat)	325,934
65B hardtop Decor Group (bucket seat)	22,226
65C hardtop standard (bench seat)	8,166
76A convertible standard (bucket seat)	38,772
76B convertible Decor Group (bucket seat)	4,845
76C convertible standard (bench seat)	1,204
Total for 1967 model year	**472,209**

1968 FORD MUSTANG PRODUCTION FIGURES

63A fastback standard (bucket seat)	33,587
63B fastback Decor Group (bucket seat)	7,661
63C fastback standard (bench seat)	1,079
63D fastback Decor Group (bench seat)	255
65A hardtop standard (bucket seat)	233,489
65B hardtop Decor Group (bucket seat)	9,012
65C hardtop standard (bench seat)	6,106
65D hardtop Decor Group (bench seat)	849
76A convertible standard (bucket seat)	22,047
76B convertible Decor Group (bucket seat)	3,338
Total for 1968 model year	**317,423**

1969 FORD MUSTANG PRODUCTION FIGURES

63A fastback standard (bucket seat)	56,025
63B fastback Decor Group (bucket seat)	5,958
63C fastback standard (Mach 1)	71,818
65A hardtop standard (bucket seat)	118,610
65B hardtop Decor Group (bucket seat)	5,208
65C hardtop standard (bench seat)	4,128
65D hardtop Decor Group (bench seat)	505
65E hardtop Grandé	22,186
76A convertible standard (bucket seat)	11,305
76B convertible Decor Group (bucket seat)	3,293
Total for 1969 model year	**299,036**

This is the cockpit of the 1969 Mach 1 up close and personal. Note the three-spoke steering wheel's rim-blow horn.

1970 FORD MUSTANG PRODUCTION FIGURES	
63A fastback standard (bucket seat)	39,491
63B fastback Decor Group (bucket seat)	6,444
63C fastback standard (Mach 1)	41,616
65A hardtop standard (bucket seat)	77,160
65B hardtop Decor Group (bucket seat)	5,408
65E hardtop Grandé	13,583
76A convertible standard (bucket seat)	6,196
76B convertible Decor Group (bucket seat)	1,624
Total for 1970 model year	**191,522**

automotive industry. People had never seen cars like them before, so novelty was a huge factor.

Another fact is that Ford ruled the road in the pony car class with just about zero competition to get in the way. One could argue that 1967–1970 Mustangs were better looking, more powerful, and had more available body trim options and equipment packages. Remember, though, GM and Mopar had offerings of their own in 1967 that were more powerful right out of the gate. It wasn't until the late 1960s that Ford had engines equal to what General Motors and Mopar offered. Combine all this with factory strikes, increasing insurance premiums and rising gas prices, then it becomes pretty clear. Make no mistake, Mustangs still ruled the day. Mustang's main competition, the Chevy Camaro, sold a respectable 824,052 units between 1967 and 1970, but that was still over 456,000 units less than Ford's pony car. Pontiac's Firebird (a veritable twin to Camaro) and Mopar's Barracuda barely made a dent in overall category sales.

Body/Chassis Construction

The 1967 through 1970 Mustangs, regardless of body style, were built on what Ford referred to as platform construction. As Ford put it:

The platform construction of the Mustang chassis is a Ford first in the American mass market. [The 1965 and 1966 Mustangs were constructed in essentially the same manner.] Based on sound engineering principles, this type of construction has many advantages and is one of the main reasons for the smooth riding characteristics and the rattle-free body of the Mustang.

The platform carries the body on the top, encloses the engine, and provides attaching points for the various chassis components. It

Remote-control mirrors received a slick chrome plate bezel in for the 1969 model year.

Primer undercoating on a 1970 Mustang Boss 429. Restorers try to get just the right overspray as the factory would have applied it.

Firewall padding and insulation was applied during restoration construction of this 1969 Mustang.

panels are pressed over, forming a wide flange, increasing front end rigidity. A one-piece stamping with a deep channel section at the top connects the inside panels across the front.

Of course, this was Ford's way of describing what was to be standard for all automotive body construction: the unibody. Keep in mind that many cars back in the day were body-on-frame construction, and the new Mustangs were decidedly different. Safer, quieter, and the way of the future!

Corrosion Protection

All 1967–1970 Mustangs received state-of-the-art corrosion protection for the era. The car's body was, according to early Ford literature, "carefully protected to retard rusting from corrosive elements and moisture. Interior body areas are vented to help prevent the entrapment of moisture. Zinclad steel is used for the body and platform members where maximum protection is required. Zinclad is a standard steel to which a heavy coating of molten zinc is applied. In all, over 20 pieces of the body and platform are of Zinclad steel. Included are the front and rear side rails, rocker panels, and body panels beneath the front and rear bumpers. In addition, zinc-rich primer is applied to lower interior portions of the various body panels, doors, pillars, and to the splash areas of the wheel housings. Asphalt-based sound deadener is sprayed on the various body and platform panels such as doors, quarter panels, and wheel housings, providing further corrosion protection."

also provides the strong basic structure, or foundation, of the car. The platform is made up of box-section front and rear side rails tied in securely to heavy boxed-in rocker panels. These components are connected by five heavy gauge crossmembers to form an extra strong ladder-type framing under the car. The front and rear side rails extend partially under and are welded to the floor pan. The full-depth, full-length tunnel down the center of the floor pan adds a backbone, giving the structure maximum rigidity. The full-depth side panels in the engine compartment are welded to the front side rails at the bottom and to the cowl at the rear. The tops of these

Body Insulation

The Ford Motor Company wanted Mustang buyers to be enjoying the smoothest, quietest cars in the market. A plethora of sound deadening and weather insulating materials were used extensively throughout the car's manufacture. Some key areas are:

- Hood: inner and outer panel construction; mastic adhesive spotted between panels
- Front fenders: inner housing, including fender apron, sprayed with sound deadener coating
- Dash panel: 1-inch-thick molded textile fiber pad with heavy plastic (vinyl) coating between passengers and engine
- Cowl sides: 1/4-inch-thick fiberglass pads at cowl sides
- Front floor area: toe-board to back of front seat with extra heavy rubberized asphalt mat sound deadener, plus thick jute pad; 1/4-inch textile fiber pad bonded to floor mat

- Rear floor area: heavy rubberized asphalt mat plus thick jute pad; ¼-inch textile fiber pad bonded to floor mat
- Door and quarter panels: sound deadener applied to inner surface of door outer panels; ½-inch textile fiber pad bonded to inner surface of quarter panel on the hardtop model
- Rear seat area: heavy rubberized asphalt mat from front of seat to back of axle kickup; seat back covered with ½-inch textile fiber padding on hardtop model
- Package tray: ¼-inch textile fiber padding under full width of package tray covering on hardtop model
- Roof panel: ½-inch fiberglass blanket insulated entire roof panel front to rear on hardtop and fastback models
- Deck lid: inner and outer construction; mastic adhesive spotted between panels
- Rear wheel housing: splash areas sprayed with sound deadener; cellulose pads between wheel housings and quarter panels for extra quietness
- Luggage compartment: floor area covered with rubber mat; ½-inch textile fiber pad bonded to top of gas tank on fastback and convertible models

Extensive use of body sealing materials included the following:
- Joint sealers: Exposed spot-welded seams and joints were protected by special plastic sealing material. Vinyl plastic sealing compound was used at roof drip rails and rear deck trough. Heat curing sealer material was applied full length to all other panel seams and joints.
- Special antisqueak and sealing devices: Special pads, grommets, seals, and plug buttons guard against friction, water, dust, and drafts. Windshields and rear window were sealed with a special nondrying plastic compound that retained its elasticity and kept a tight seal. Plastic shields covered the inside surfaces of door trim panels to prevent water damage.

Assembly and Body Construction

The 1967 through 1970 Mustangs were all assembled in the same manner. The all-welded body assembly was designed and engineered to provide maximum strength with minimum weight. The body was welded to the platform-type chassis for maximum durability and a solid overall feel.

Aside from the basic design differences in the roof B- and C-pillar area, the bodies of all

Mustangs were pretty much identical. All of the framing around the bodies' openings and roof bracings on the hardtop and fastback (2+2) were of either the box-channel or hat-section design. The double-walled upper cowl and the instrument panel were welded to the body structure to provide extra strength and rigidity. The front fenders were bolted to the body for ease in replacing.

It's in the Codes and Their Locations

All 1967–1970 Mustangs came from the factory with a vehicle identification number (VIN) and a trim/DSO code affixed. As the years progressed, the location and method of application of identification differed.

The series of numbers after the engine designation reflected each individual car's consecutive unit number. Consecutive unit numbers were assigned upon vehicle order and plugged into the production schedule at that time.

The distinct body and trim codes, paint codes, date of manufacture, axle and transmission codes, and DSOs were also noted on the ID plate. These aspects for each individual year will be covered in their respective chapters.

This restoration of a 1969 Mustang shows how the unibody is constructed.

1967: The VIN was stamped into the top of the inner fender like the 1965 and 1966 Mustangs. The identification (ID) plate containing the VIN and the trim/DSO code was also riveted to the outer edge of the driver's door.

1968: The VIN and the trim/DSO codes were all on the ID plate riveted to the outer edge of the driver's door.

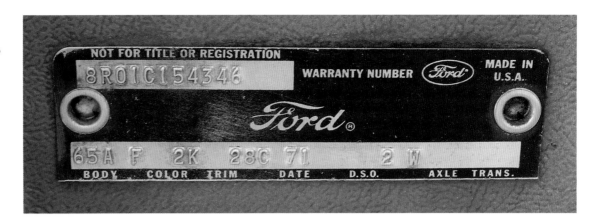

HOW TO DECIPHER THE VEHICLE IDENTIFICATION NUMBER (VIN) ON 1967–1970 MUSTANGS

- The first digit of the VIN designates the model year of the car:
  7= 1967, 8=1968, 9=1969, 0=1970

- The second letter indicates the assembly plant:
  F= Dearborn, Michigan
  R= San Jose, California
  T= Metuchen, New Jersey

- The third and fourth digits designate the body style:
  01= hardtop
  02= fastback
  03= convertible

- The fifth letter designates the engine size:
  A= 289-ci eight-cylinder, 4 bbl
  C= 289-ci eight-cylinder, 2 bbl
  F= 302-ci eight-cylinder, 2 bbl
  G= 302-ci eight-cylinder, 4 bbl (Boss 302)
  H= 351-ci eight-cylinder, 2 bbl
  J= 302-ci eight-cylinder, 4 bbl (1968 only)
  K= 289-ci eight-cylinder, 4 bbl (high performance)
  L= 250-ci six-cylinder, 1 bbl
  M= 351-ci eight-cylinder, 4 bbl
  Q= 428-ci eight-cylinder, 4 bbl (non-Ram Air)
  R= 428-ci eight-cylinder, 4 bbl (Ram Air, midyear intro, 1968)
  S= 390-ci eight-cylinder, 4 bbl
  T= 200-ci six-cylinder, 1 bbl
  W= 427-ci eight-cylinder, 4 bbl (early 1968 only)
  Z= 429-ci eight-cylinder, 4 bbl (Boss 429)

1969: The VIN was stamped into a metal plate and affixed to the outmost edge of the dash pad, where it could easily be seen through the windshield on the driver's side. The ID plate containing the VIN and the trim/DSO code was also riveted to the outer edge of the driver's door.

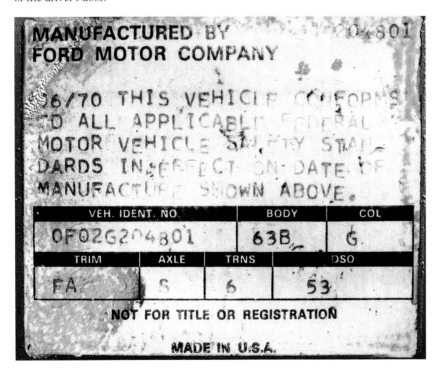

ABOVE: Here's something you don't see every day: a double stamp of the VIN. After the 1967 model year, the VIN stamping on Mustang's inner fenderwell was discontinued. LEFT: 1970: Carried over from the 1969 model year, the VIN was stamped into a metal plate and affixed to the outmost edge of the dash pad, where it could easily be seen through the windshield on the driver's side. The metal ID plate was discarded in favor of a laminated sticker on the driver's door edge.

By the Numbers

Every part affixed to the 1967–1970 Mustangs had a part number stamped into the metal, cast into the iron, molded into the plastic, or stamped in ink or paint. This ranged from a metal tag affixed to rear differential housing, a part number cast in an intake manifold, a number molded into a taillight lens, or an ID code silk-screened onto a voltage regulator.

During the mid- to late-1960s, Mustang production was at an all-time high. The three assembly plants in Dearborn, San Jose, and Metuchen were working at break-neck speeds trying to keep up with production. Quite often, in order to keep up with demand, Ford overproduced many parts. Most of the time this worked, but some of the time parts were produced and stockpiled. This led to things like 1968 Mustangs with "67" molded into the taillight lens, and 1970 cars with 1969 coding stamped into various chassis components. Generally speaking, the dates associated with the parts on late 1960s Mustangs corresponded to within two or three months of the cars' build dates identified on the vehicles' ID plates.

Considering the vastness of Mustang production, Ford's parts numbering system was, for the most part, very accurate and did the job. Most part numbers even identified the month and day of their "born on" date. As various parts and accessories were built by outside suppliers, they were accounted for and coded with various bits of information that plugged directly into Ford's own network. Each of the three different manufacturing facilities located throughout the United States leaned heavily on its own local industries for the outsourcing and quality of numerous items.

Although this book will decipher many codes and numbers throughout the following chapters, there isn't enough space here to list every Ford part and application. For further complete information on this subject, I recommend purchasing a shop manual or parts identifier. An excellent guide to the complete small-block V-8 engine and engine parts number system is *Mustang & Ford Small-Block V-8 1962–1969* by Bob Mannel.

Although I will attempt to produce a comprehensive and accurate listing of many parts and options for 1967–1970 Mustangs, this book should not be used as a sole source of part or casting identification.

This photo shows an Autolite branded voltage regulator affixed to the inner fender well. Autolife was a subsidiary company of FoMoCo. The part number and application indentification was silk-screened on to the other housing.

Alternator housing and brackets had the Ford part number, year, and application literally cast into the steel substrate. This feature is easily indentifiable on the production line, as well as in the aftermarket world.

The Thermactor air bypass valve is part of the emission controls. This unit on a Boss 429 was indentified with a part number printed to a label and affixed to the part.

Part numbers were printed on the air cleaner, silk-screened on the spark plug wires (although in this case they are modern wires), and stamped into the export bracing.

CASTING NUMBER BREAKDOWN

The following casting number breakdown shows how Ford Motor Company identified many of its parts.

Decade of Manufacture
A= 1940
B= 1950
C= 1960
D= 1970

Year of Decade
The year of the decade was determined by adding a number between zero and nine to the letter of the decade. Example: C6=1966

Car Line
A= Galaxie
D= Falcon
F= Outside United States
G= Comet/Montego
J= Industrial
M= Mercury
O= Fairlane/Torino
P= Autolite/Motorcraft
R= Rotunda
S= Thunderbird
T= Truck
V= Lincoln
Z= Mustang

Engineering Departments
A= chassis
B= body
E= engine
F= engine accessories
P= automatic transmission
R= manual transmission
W= axle
X= Muscle Parts Program
Y= Lincoln Mercury Service Parts
Z= Ford Service Parts

ABOVE: The upper radiator hose is ink stamped with Autolite branding, part number, and application.

LEFT: The 1968 rear side marker reflector lens is stamped with FoMoCo indentification, as well as the part number and year.

Chapter 2

1967

When Chevrolet introduced their new Camaro for the 1967 model year, it was undoubtedly a success. The styling was crisp and compact, and it looked ready to compete with the first generation Mustangs. Ford had completely restyled its pony car for the 1967 model year, and the car looked years ahead of Camaro by comparison.

Ford had designed the second generation Mustangs to look more aggressive, but still unmistakably

Mustang. The new cars were longer and wider by a couple of inches in each direction. Height was almost identical to the 1965–1966 cars, but with the wider stance they appeared lower. Wheelbase remained the same at 108 inches.

The fanfare was huge with the intro of the "next" pony car. Ford had plenty of time to plan out the new car and jumped right out of the gate with all three models (hardtop, fastback, and

OPPOSITE & ABOVE:
A spectacular 1967
Mustang GT-A (for
automatic transmission)
convertible in
Wimbledon White. The
Tennessee license plate
says it all! *Tom Shaw*

RIGHT: Retail sales
brochure for the "All-
New for '67" Mustang.

Three new ways to answer the call of the Mustang...

Mustang '67

Take the Mustang pledge! This full-page, full-color ad appeared in *Look* magazine for 1967.

The base Mustang hardtop for 1967 still looks great, even in the no-frills version! *Tom Shaw*

convertible). It was a big step for Ford, considering that the previous model year (1966) had sold a record-setting 607,568 units, but it was a step in the right direction.

How do you make a great car even greater? The first step is to give it more power, of course! Ford knew that with the onslaught of General Motors (GM) and Mopar competition a power struggle loomed on the horizon. It made sure the new Mustang was wide enough to accept big-block power. Although traditional muscle cars had been around for a few years, the pony car wars were just beginning. Consumers were demanding more power from their vehicles, and by 1967 cars like Chevelle, GTO, Fairlane, and GTX were all packed with over-the-top firepower. If Ford had rested on its laurels and run with the first generation body style one more year, it would have been a massive error in judgment. FoMoCo did

it up right and continued to set the world on fire. By the end of the 1967 model year, 472,209 Mustangs had rolled out of the three assembly plants. The new Camaro, for all its hype, didn't meet half that total. Chevrolet sold 220,917 versions of its pony car. It was respectable, but Ford still ruled with an iron fist.

Three new ways to answer the call of the Mustang . . .

Mustang's sexy retail sales brochure was a full-color, 16-page, high-gloss piece packed with photos and illustrations proclaiming Mustang as king. Open the first page, and the sales pitch started:

How do you improve on a classic? How do you add excitement to an American original—an original that is already the most exciting, most acclaimed new car in history? With subtle body changes and interior improvements, the

OPPOSITE: A Mustang convertible for 1967 in Candyapple Red. Styled steel wheels were optional equipment.

A 1967 Mustang hardtop in Lime Gold. Redline tires are not stock equipment, but many people added them as aftermarket options.

The Mustang GT fastback for 1967 poses at the Columbia River Gorge.

ABOVE & OPPOSITE: The gorgeous 1967 GTA hardtop in Silver Frost with a black vinyl top. BELOW: The 1967 GT fog lights are all lit up and ready for prime time!

result is a rare combination that says Mustang for 1967 is undeniably new—without taking away the flair and flavor of the classic design that is so unmistakably Mustang!

We've added fresh Mustang optional features, like a hefty 390-ci Thunderbird Special V-8 for extra spirit. Like the Tilt-Away Steering Wheel that moves aside when you open the door and tilts up and down to nine different driving positions. Fingertip Speed Control, which lets you set cruising speed without need to maintain constant accelerator pressure.

These body buck tags were used to provide instructions to assembly line workers so that special options, special orders, and build exceptions could be noted on each vehicle. There is a small hole punched in the tag, right over the 2T, which was how an assembly line worker acknowledged the instructions by randomly punching these holes.

SelectShift Cruise-O-Matic . . . go fully automatic or shift manually for the fun of it without a clutch. Greater traction Wide-Oval Sports Tires with V-8s. Front Power Disc Brakes. SelectAire Conditioner and Convenience Control Panel.

What did we keep? The standards that made Mustang a classic in the first place . . . standards that won the hearts of almost a million and a half owners in under three years. Those owners (and many more) have taken the Mustang Pledge . . . because of standard features like bucket seats and full carpeting. Floor-mounted shift. All-vinyl trim. Lithe performance and handling. And most particularly we kept the classic long, lean, adventurous look of Mustang, the original. Take the Mustang Pledge in one of three exciting ways . . . hardtop, convertible, fastback.

Ford just couldn't help adding a big, bold sign offline: "Bred first . . . to be first!"

Total 1967 Mustang production saw 472,209 units, of which 356,326 were hardtops; 71,062 were fastbacks; and 44,821 were convertibles. See table in Chapter 1 for complete individual model production listing.

Body, Models, and Exterior Trim

The GTA for 1967 received GT side stripes and styled steel wheels.

Although the all-new-for-1967 Mustang was literally "all new," the three basic models and body styles continued on from the 1965–1966 cars. The hardtop, fastback 2+2, and convertible all held true to their original form and offered the consumers exciting good looks, no matter which style they chose.

The hardtop sold a staggering 356,326 units and proved to be the most popular model by far. At a base price $2,461.46, the new hardtop was only $45 more than the previous 1966 model.

The fastback was perhaps the most notably different body style with its long sloping back glass area. The look was described as gran turismo and aggressive. The fastback carried a base price sticker of $2,592.17—a far cry from what one would sell for today!

The convertible was clearly the best looking of the three models with its low, wide stance. The dimensions were the same for all Mustangs in 1967, but with the top down, the convertible

ABOVE: Convertible tops for 1967 were available in Black or White only. BELOW: Simulated air side scoops were standard on all Mustangs for 1967.

This emblem reflects the "big dog" powerplant for 1967. It was the first year of big-block power in Mustang!

looked lower, thus it added to its dramatic new lines. The base price was $2,698.14.

Exterior Styling and Features

All three models carried on the tradition of Mustang benchmark and, once again, received the now-classic long-hood and short-deck treatment. Highlights include:

- Deeply inset grille with a crisp mesh appearance accentuated the long length of the hood. The familiar "corralled" Mustang ornament was positioned at grille center. The entire grille was outlined with bright metal moldings.
- New radial spoke design wheel covers were added.
- Highly sculptured bodyside panels that terminated with twin simulated air scoops added emphasis to the low, long look.
- Full-length bright rocker panel molding was standard.
- F-O-R-D lettering on the hood leading edge, M-U-S-T-A-N-G lettering and emblem on the front fenders, and M-U-S-T-A-N-G lettering on the deck lid provided attractive product identification.
- Windshield, recessed rear window, and curved side windows were tastefully outlined with bright metal trim.
- Three bright metal-trimmed taillights/turn signals were located at either side of the concave rear body panel.
- Standard-equipment back-up lights were

The Mustang GT grille for 1967. Note the deep "pony" and "corral" moldings. This changed to a shallower version for 1968.

LEFT: The pop-open gas cap was part of the Exterior Decor Group for 1967. GT-equipped Mustangs have the GT emblem.

BELOW: Early 1967 Mustangs featured individual letters designating "M-U-S-T-A-N-G" on the fenders. Later versions switched to script. The emblem did not show engine callout on six-cylinder cars.

below the bumper in the lower valance panel.

- The styled fuel filler cap (still located in the center of the rear taillight panel) featured three-blade knockoff design with a Mustang emblem displayed at center.
- On convertible models, the convertible top was five-ply vinyl and available in black or white. The top boot was all vinyl and color-keyed to the interior.

The GT Equipment Group ($205.05) could be ordered on any Mustang equipped with one of the four V-8 engines. For the 1967 model year, GTs equipped with an automatic transmission received special labeling in the stripe that ran the bottom length of the car. The emblem read "GTA," with the "A" denoting the automatic transmission. The GT Equipment Group had the following: 4-inch driving lamps mounted inside the grille; power front disc brakes; a low-restriction dual exhaust system with chromed quad exhaust tips that exited from cutouts in the rear valance panel; GT rocker panel striping; GT emblem on gas cap; and a special handling package that included higher rate springs and shocks and a larger-diameter front stabilizer bar.

The Exterior Decor Group ($38.86) came with bright wheel lip opening moldings, a hood

The lower back grille was a $12.95 option on Mustang for 1967. It certainly added distinction.

ABOVE: Hood louvers with turn-signal indicators were part of the Exterior Decor Group for 1967.

RIGHT: Backup lights were standard equipment on all Mustang models.

Vinyl tops were finished off with a beautiful set of stainless steel moldings.

Not known for its huge cargo capacity, Mustang trunks were just big enough for the bare essentials.

with functional rear-facing louvers and integrated turn signal lamps, bright rear deck moldings on hardtops and convertibles (but was standard trim on fastback models), and a pop-open fuel filler cap. A special lower back panel grille ($19.48) was available for all models equipped with the Exterior Decor Group.

A vinyl top was offered for the hardtop model Mustangs and was available in two colors only—black and parchment.

1967 STANDARD EQUIPMENT

- Accelerator pedal: suspended type
- Alternator: 38 amps
- Armrests: front, energy absorbing
- Armrests: rear, ashtrays (convertible only)
- Ashtray: front
- Backup lights
- Battery: Sta-Ful design
- Body: rust resistant
- Brakes: self adjusting, dual system
- Bucket seats: foam padded, adjustable
- Carpets: nylon/rayon, molded
- Choke: automatic
- Cigarette lighter
- Coat hooks
- Coolant: two years or 36,000 miles
- Courtesy lights: door switches
- Curved side glass
- Door checks: two stages
- Door hinges: bronze, bushed
- Door latches: bear-hug
- Door trim: all vinyl
- Emergency flashers
- Engine: 200 Six
- Finish: Super Diamond Lustre Enamel
- Front fenders: bolt-on
- Fuel tank: 16 gallons
- Glass: safety
- Glove box: instrument panel mounted
- Headlining: color-keyed vinyl (hardtop and fastback only)
- Heater and defroster: fresh air
- Hood latch: single action
- Horns: dual
- Instrument panel: padded
- Insulated body
- Jack: scissors type, body side
- Lamps, bulbs: extended life
- Lubrication, chassis: 36,000 miles
- Maintenance: twice a year
- Mirror: inside rearview, day/night
- Mirror: outside rearview
- Molding: rocker panel
- Muffler: aluminized
- Scuff plates: aluminum
- Seat belt: deluxe front and rear with reminder light
- Steering wheel: deep dish, safety type
- Sun visors: padded, color-keyed
- Thermostat: 195 degrees Fahrenheit
- Transmission: three-speed manual
- Transmission lever: tunnel mounted
- Turn signals
- Upholstery: all-vinyl
- Valve lifters: hydraulic
- Ventilation: Cowl-Aire intakes (hardtop and convertible only)
- Ventilation: Cowl-Aire plus roof vent outlets (fastback only)
- Wheel covers: full
- Windshield washers
- Windshield wipers: 15-inch electric, two speeds

BODY SPECIFICATIONS

	Hardtop	Fastback	Convertible
Length (inches, overall)	183.6	183.6	183.6
Width (inches, overall)	70.9	70.9	70.9
Height (inches, overall)	51.6	51.6	51.6
Wheelbase (inches)	108	108	108
Curb weight (pounds)	2,696	2,723	2,856
(six-cylinder, standard transmission)			

VIN/TRIM/DSO TAG DECODING FOR 1967

Model Year Code
7= 1967

Assembly Plant Codes
F= Dearborn, Michigan
R= San Jose, California
T= Metuchen, New Jersey

Body Serial Codes
01= hardtop
02= fastback
03= convertible

Engine Codes
A= 289-ci eight-cylinder, 4 bbl
C= 289-ci eight-cylinder, 2 bbl
K= 289-ci eight-cylinder, 4 bbl (high performance)
S= 390-ci eight-cylinder, 4 bbl
T= 200-ci six-cylinder, 1 bbl

Consecutive Number
The remaining six digits in the VIN indicate the vehicle's consecutive unit number assigned at the production line.

BODY STYLE CODES

63A= fastback standard (bucket seat)
63B= fastback Decor Group (bucket seat)
63C= fastback standard (bench seat)
65A= hardtop standard (bucket seat)
65B= hardtop Decor Group (bucket seat)
65C= hardtop standard (bench seat)
76A= convertible standard (bucket seat)
76B= convertible Decor Group (bucket seat)
76C= convertible standard (bench seat)

COLOR CODES

4= Silver Frost	6= Pebble Beige
8= Springtime Yellow	A= Raven Black
B= Frost Turquoise	E= Beige Mist
I= Lime Gold	K= Nightmist Blue
M= Wimbledon White	Q= Brittany Blue
T= Candyapple Red	V= Burnt Amber
W= Clearwater Aqua	X= Vintage Burgundy
Y= Dark Moss Green	Z= Sauterne Gold

TRIM CODES

Standard Bucket Seats
2A= Black 2B= Blue 2D= Red 2F= Saddle 2G= Ivy Gold 2K= Aqua
2U= Parchment

Interior Decor Group (Bucket Seats)
6A= Black 6B= Blue 6D= Red 6F= Saddle 6G= Ivy Gold 6K= Aqua
6U= Parchment

TRIM CODES (CTD)

Bench Seat
4A= Black 4U= Parchment

Standard Bucket Seats (with Comfortweave Option)
7A= Black 7U= Parchment

Interior Decor Group (with Comfortweave Option)
5A= Black 5U= Parchment

DATE CODES

The number (1–31) appearing before the month letter indicates the day.

Month	First Year	Second Year
January	A	N
February	B	P
March	C	Q
April	D	R
May	E	S
June	F	T
July	G	U
August	H	V
September	J	W
October	K	X
November	L	Y
December	M	Z

DSO CODES

This code indicates the city/state in which the vehicle was originally destined for delivery.

11= Boston, Massachusetts	13= New York City, New York
15= Newark, New Jersey	16= Philadelphia, Pennsylvania
17= Washington, D.C.	21= Atlanta, Georgia
22= Charlotte, North Carolina	24= Jacksonville, Florida
25= Richmond, Virginia	27= Cincinnati, Ohio
28= Louisville, Kentucky	32= Cleveland, Ohio
33= Detroit, Michigan	34= Indianapolis, Indiana
35= Lansing, Michigan	37= Buffalo, New York
38= Pittsburgh, Pennsylvania	41= Chicago, Illinois
42= Fargo, North Dakota	43= Milwaukee, Wisconsin
44= Twin Cities, Minnesota	45= Davenport, Iowa
51= Denver, Colorado	52= Des Moines, Iowa
53= Kansas City, Missouri	54= Omaha, Nebraska
55= St. Louis, Missouri	61= Dallas, Texas
62= Houston, Texas	63= Memphis, Tennessee
64= New Orleans, Louisiana	65= Oklahoma City, Oklahoma
71= Los Angeles, California	72= San Jose, California
73= Salt Lake City, Utah	74= Seattle, Washington
75= Phoenix, Arizona	81= Ford of Canada
83= Government	84= Home Office Reserve
85= American Red Cross	89= Transportation Services
90–99= Export	

AXLE CODES

Conventional	Limited Slip	Axle Ratio
0		3.10
1	A	3.00
2	B	2.83
3	C	3.20
4	D	3.25
5	E	3.50
6	F	2.80
8	G	2.75
9	H	4.11

TRANSMISSION CODES

1= three-speed manual
U= automatic (C6)
5= four-speed manual
W= automatic (C4)

The base Mustang interior for 1967 is shown in Saddle (2F). *Tom Shaw*

Interior

With the complete overhaul of the new 1967 Mustang exterior came a slick new look for the interior. Actually the changes made to the inside of the new car weren't as dramatic as those made on the outside. Refinement is a more apt description. Ford's sale literature described it perfectly:

- All-new sports styled interior with foam-padded twin bucket seats
- New door trim panels with horizontal pleated design, trimmed with bright Mylar moldings
- Choice of seven all-vinyl trims—Black, Blue, Red, Saddle, Ivy Gold, Aqua, and Parchment
- New instrument panel and cluster: large, easy to read gauges for fuel, oil pressure, amps, and temperature.
- Large, pullout ashtray with concealed cigarette lighter
- All major items, including the headlining, color-keyed to the interior trim selection
- New dome light with door-operated courtesy switches

- Additional standard equipment features: 16-inch, three-spoke steering wheel; long-wearing nylon-rayon carpeting molded to the floor contour; suspended accelerator pedal; and front seat armrests

Aside from the obvious styling touches and new standard interior features, Ford expanded Mustang's standard safety package. The interior of the new Mustangs included an impact-absorbing steering wheel with oversize, deep padded hub. The newly designed center hub was engineered to progressively collapse on impact. Hub construction consisted of urethane foam surrounded by polyvinylchloride and encased in vinyl. All Mustangs were equipped with deluxe push-button-release front and rear seatbelts, with retractors on the front hubs. A reminder light on the instrument panel glowed from 7 to 10 seconds each time the ignition switch was turned on. Safety padding manufactured from specially formulated foam material was attached to the top of all Mustang instrument panels.

Ford developed the armrests to provide further protection against lateral impact injuries.

The armrest design consisted of a honeycomb-type core surrounded and filled with foam and encased in vinyl. The honeycomb was positioned vertically to give the necessary strength, but would collapse laterally on impact. It was standard on all Mustangs except those with the Interior Decor option. Visor padding was specially formulated for extra energy-absorbing properties. The Day/Nite rearview mirror was encased in a vinyl frame and firmly bonded to the backing, which held the fragments together if it was ever broken. The outside remote-control rearview mirror was formerly an option, but was standard in 1967. Padded windshield pillars were a new feature in 1967 and consisted of moldings of energy-absorbing foam covered with low-gloss color-keyed vinyl.

The new 1967 instrument panel carried over the first generation Mustangs hooded theme, but improved it by slightly rounding the hoods. However, the gauge layout was completely different than on the earlier cars. The new gauges consisted of two large pods and three smaller pods. The large pod on the left housed a speedometer that went to 120 miles per hour, and the pod on the right was reserved for the oil pressure and alternator gauges. The three smaller pods housed the fuel gauge to the extreme left; clock in the

ABOVE: High zoot Interior Decor Group pictured in Red (6D). *Tom Shaw*

LEFT: Interior Decor Group seats featured chrome buttons in seat backs for 1967.

OPPOSITE: Driver's view of the Interior Decor Group for 1967. C'mon in! *Tom Shaw*

center, if the option was included; and a temperature gauge in the right pod.

The Interior Decor Group ($108.06 and $94.36 for the convertible) boosted the luxury level of the Mustang considerably. It included:
• Custom inner door panels with a brushed aluminum panel appliqué and molded-in armrests

The convertible top boot is color-keyed to the body color.

BELOW:The AM/FM radio was integrated into the top of the console.

BOTTOM: This 120 mph speedometer came standard on all Mustangs. Note the "red line" starts at 70 mph

- A unique grille section affixed to the lower door, which had courtesy lights
- Special brushed aluminum inserts on the instrument panel
- Special molded seat backs with side shields
- Insert trim buttons on the seat backs
- Padded trim panels (hardtop only)
- A roof console with twin reading lights and switches (not available on convertible)
- Vinyl grip on automatic transmission lever (Cruise-O-Matic only)
- Bright trim surrounds on the brake and clutch (if so equipped) pedals
- Electric clock
- Padded trim panels (hardtop only)

Other interior options for 1967 are listed here: a full-width bench seat; seatbelt for a third passenger; speed control; Comfortweave vinyl trim (knitted vinyl seat inserts); front shoulder harness; fold-down rear seat (fastback model only); tachometer (6,000 rpm available on all models and 8,000 rpm on models equipped with 289 Hi-Po engine); SelectAire air conditioning; center console; convenience control panel; courtesy light group; tilt steering wheel; deluxe steering wheel; AM radio; AM/FM radio; and stereosonic tape/AM radio. For a complete listing of all options, see the options chart in this chapter.

Chassis

As described in Chapter 1, "The platform carries the body on the top, encloses the engine, and provides attaching points for the various chassis components. It also provides the basic structure of the car. The platform is made up of a box-section front and rear side rails tied in securely to heavy

The Interior Decor Group in all its glory. Note the appointments in brushed aluminum.

BELOW: Courtesy door lights in decorative trim came with the Interior Decor Group.

BOTTOM: A molded roof console with map lights was part of the Interior Decor Group on hardtops and fastbacks.

boxed-in rocker panels. These components are connected by five heavy gauge crossmembers to form an extra strong ladder-type framing under the car. The front and rear side rails extend partially under, and are welded to, the floor pan. The full-depth, full-length tunnel down the center of the floor pan adds a backbone and gives the structure maximum rigidity. The full-depth side panels in the engine compartment are welded to the front side rails at the bottom and to the cowl at the rear. The tops of these panels are pressed over to form a wide flange and increase front end rigidity. A one-piece stamping with a deep channel section at the top connects the inside panels across the front."

Regardless of the car's engine size, all Mustangs were based on the same platform chassis. Upgraded suspension components compensated for the weight differences in engines.

Engines

Ford's "little workhorse" was standard equipment on all Mustang models for 1967. As Ford stated in its early sales literature: "This exceptional six-cylinder engine has been further refined for 1967 to give greater efficiency, better low speed operation, and continued good cold starting characteristics.

"The seven main bearing crankshaft has been an outstanding feature of the engine that is retained for 1967. The use of seven main bearings provides extra smooth operation and long life durability.

The 289-ci A-code (four-barrel) engine has been dressed up with the following nonstock items: chrome air cleaner, Cobra valve covers, high-performance spark plug wires, and a Monte Carlo–style export brace.

BASE EQUIPMENT ENGINE: T-CODE

- Bore and stroke: 3.68x3.13
- Carburetor: Autolite 1100, 1V
- Compression ratio: 9.2:1
- Displacement: 200 ci
- Horsepower: 120 at 4,400 rpm
- Torque: 190 ft-lbs at 2,400 rpm
- Type: inline six-cylinder, overhead valve
- Valve lifters: hydraulic

OPPOSITE: The Six was standard equipment in all Mustang models for 1967. The engine put out 120 horsepower and 190 ft-lbs of torque. *Tom Shaw*

"Hydraulic valve lifters ensure quiet, low maintenance operation of the oversize valves. The automatic choke is the dual sensing type which minimizes the chances of flooding a semi-warm engine."

Quick facts:

- Seven main bearings: smoother engine operation, less vibration, longer engine life
- Hydraulic valve lifters: quiet operation, low maintenance
- Large valves: more efficient breathing, more seat area for better cooling, and less burning
- Short-stroke design: less vibration, less wear
- Single-venturi carburetor: economical operation
- Six-month or 6,000-mile oil filter: reduced maintenance, improved oil filtering

- Automatic choke: sensed ambient and coolant temperatures; helped prevent flooding on semiwarm starts
- Compression ratio of 9.2:1: better efficiency on regular or economy gasoline
- Thin wall casting: better cooling, less weight
- Precision-molded crankshaft: dependable, smooth operation
- Weather-insulated ignition system: reliable starts under all climatic conditions

289-ci V-8 2V

The two-barrel Challenger V-8 was the base V-8 engine for Mustang, and as Ford put it in 1967: "A number of important refinements have been made for 1967 to this most popular Ford V-8 engine. Under the redesigned rocker arm covers, a new valve train is introduced to improve reliability and durability while cutting maintenance intervals. New rocker arms are guided by the valves themselves, thus cutting down on close tolerances. Redesigned low inertia valve springs aid performance while cutting down on wear. In addition to this, overall performance has been improved by adding a new two-venturi carburetor."

Quick facts:

- Lightweight cast-iron construction: used advanced thin wall casting techniques

The 390-ci four-barrel GT engine. This was the first ever big-block engine stuffed into a Mustang. With a horsepower rating of 320 at 4,800 rpm, the car has ample power! *Tom Shaw*

OPTIONAL EQUIPMENT ENGINE: C-CODE (CHALLENGER)

- Bore and stroke: 4.00x2.87
- Carburetor: Autolite 2100 (280 cfm), 2V
- Compression ratio: 9.3:1
- Displacement: 289 ci
- Horsepower: 200 at 4,400 rpm
- Torque: 282 ft-lbs at 2,400 rpm
- Type: eight cylinder, overhead valve
- Valve lifters: hydraulic

- Short-stroke design: less friction, longer engine life
- Full-length, full-circle water jackets: uniform cylinder temperature with a minimum of hot spots
- Autothermic piston design: maintained critical clearances required for smooth efficiency
- Hydraulic valve lifters: no adjustment required
- Automatic choke: sensed ambient and coolant temperatures; helped prevent flooding on semiwarm starts
- Two-venturi carburetor: newly designed for improved economy and performance.
- High-capacity fuel filter: in-line design to provide maximum filtration

- Six-month or 6,000-mile oil filter: reduced maintenance, improved oil filtering
- Autolite power tip spark plugs: self-cleaning, extralong firing tip
- Dual advance distributor: correct spark advance for all driving conditions

289-ci V-8 4V

Mustang's base four-barrel V-8 was a popular option for those wanting a little more zoot in their 'Stangs. Ford tells us: "This engine is designed to extract the most power from premium fuels and develops 225 horsepower at 4,800 rpm. Similar in design to the 289 2V engine, the differences include revised valve timing, higher compression ratio, and piston design similar to that used in the High-Performance 289 V-8. The special ignition system insures the necessary spark characteristics needed to give exciting performance with reasonable economy. Also added to the 1967 model of this engine is the Autolite modified Air-Valve carburetor. This engine features the alternate intake and exhaust valves, which improve volumetric efficiency and virtually eliminate hot spots which are common when exhaust valves are side by side."

Quick facts:
- Low tension piston rings: reduced wear and provided positive sealing

The magnificent 390-ci four-barrel V-8. The first year that the big-block engine appeared in Mustang's was 1967. Chrome value covers and the top of the air cleaner helped set off the visual clues.

OPTIONAL EQUIPMENT ENGINE: A-CODE

- Bore and stroke: 4.00x2.87
- Carburetor: Autolite 4100 (480 cfm), 4V
- Compression ratio: 9.8:1
- Displacement: 289 ci
- Horsepower: 225 at 4,800 rpm
- Torque: 305 ft-lbs at 3,200 rpm
- Type: eight cylinder, overhead valve
- Valve lifters: hydraulic

- Compression ratio of 9.8:1: permitted most effective use of premium fuels
- Alternate valve spacing: higher volumetric efficiency, elimination of hot spots in the cylinder block and head
- Lightweight cast-iron construction: used advanced thin wall casting techniques
- New Autolite 4V carburetor: modified Air-Valve design for high efficiency
- Short-stroke design: less friction, longer engine life
- Thirty-six-thousand-mile air filter: high filtration with low maintenance
- High-capacity fuel filter: inline design to provide maximum filtration
- Full-length, full-circle water jackets: uniform

cylinder temperature with a minimum of hot spots
- Autothermic piston design: maintained critical clearances required for smooth efficiency
- Six-month or 6,000-mile oil filter: reduced maintenance, improved oil filtering
- Dual advance distributor: correct spark advance for all driving conditions

289-ci V-8 4V High-Performance

The 1967 model year was the last year for the famed High-Performance 289 in the Mustang. Bigger, more powerful engines were right around the corner. Ford describes the 289 Hi-Po in its sales literature for 1967:

The engine is available with either the manual four-speed transmission or a heavy-duty three-speed Cruise-O-Matic automatic transmission. With its advanced engineering design and precision thin wall castings, this engine puts out 0.95 horsepower per cubic inch and weighs only 2 pounds per horsepower for unsurpassed performance in its class.

On the intake side, it features a low restriction, racing type air cleaner, a special large bore, four-venturi carburetor, and large passages in the intake manifold and cylinder

The big 600 cfm Holley carburetor was standard when the 390 V-8 was ordered in 1967.

This photo shows the correct placement of the air cleaner decals on the 390 V-8.

OPTIONAL EQUIPMENT ENGINE: K-CODE (HI-PO)

- Bore and stroke: 4.00x2.87
- Carburetor: Autolite 4100 (480 cfm), 4V
- Compression ratio: 10.5:1
- Displacement: 289 ci
- Horsepower: 271 at 6,000 rpm
- Torque: 312 lbs-ft at 3,400 rpm
- Type: eight cylinder, overhead valve
- Valve lifters: solid

heads—all designed for free breathing and high volumetric efficiency. Solid valve lifters, a special camshaft with greater valve timing overlap, and a beefed-up rocker arm system provide the necessary valve action for high rpm operation. The high compression cylinder heads and special pistons utilize all the power available in the premium fuel that is required for good operation."

Quick facts:

- Free-flow exhaust system: large exhaust passages, individual exhaust header to minimize exhaust pressure, twin pipes and mufflers
- High strength connecting rods: beefed up for safety and performance
- Chrome-plated valve stems: anticorrosion, long life, reduced friction
- Compression ratio of 10.0:1: maximum power from premium fuels

- Solid valve lifters: precise valve action at high rpm
- High-performance camshaft: specially contoured for high lift valve opening and greater valve overlap
- Racing-type air cleaner: low restriction for maximum efficiency under high-speed conditions
- Special ignition system: centrifugal advance distributor
- Thirty-six-thousand-mile air filter: high filtration with low maintenance
- High-capacity fuel filter: inline design to provide maximum filtration
- Short stroke design: less friction, longer engine life

- Lightweight, cast-iron construction: uses advanced, thin wall casting techniques
- Alternate valve spacing: higher volumetric efficiency, elimination of hot spots in cylinder block and heads

390-ci V-8 4V

Mustang's first year with big-block was 1967. The Thunderbird Special V-8 seemed like it was made to order for the newly restyled, wider Mustangs. There was a 315-horsepower version of this engine for the Thunderbird, and the 320 versions were selected for Mustang and Fairlanes. Ford said, "The 320-horsepower version gets its extra power from a new high speed camshaft; modified valve springs; a larger carburetor (Autolite Air-Valve); a special distributor; and a low restriction, racing-type air filter. For 1967, carburetor refinements will provide great economy and improved cold engine operation."

Quick facts:
- Chrome dress-up kit: standard on the 320 horsepower version with chrome-plated air cleaner, valve covers, oil filter, dip stick, and radiator cap
- Full-flow fuel filter: inline design to provide maximum filtration
- High-performance valve springs and damper assembly: greater resistance to fatigue and wear
- Six-month or 6,000-mile oil filter: reduced maintenance, improved oil filtering
- Compression ratio of 10.5:1: maximum power from premium fuels
- New camshaft lobe profile: more usable torque with a smooth idle.
- Dual advance distributor: correct spark advance for all driving conditions
- Lightweight, cast-iron construction: used advanced thin wall casting techniques
- Alternate valve spacing: higher volumetric efficiency, elimination of hot spots in cylinder block and heads
- Free-flow exhaust system: large exhaust passages, individual exhaust header to minimize exhaust pressure, twin pipes and mufflers
- Short stroke design: less friction, longer engine life

SelectShift Cruise-O-Matic transmission was a fully automatic unit. The unit permitted manual shifting as well as shiftless driving.

- Low-capacity oil sump: four-quart design giving better circulation and cooling

Transmissions

For 1967, the base transmission was the three-speed manual. This was a fully synchronized unit and was standard equipment with all engines, except the 289 high-performance V-8.

A four-speed manual transmission was optional with all engines except the 200-ci six-cylinder. Ford described the transmission as "fully synchronized in all forward gears, permitting upshifts and downshifts at reasonable car speeds without gear clash or noise." When the transmission was ordered with the 289 high-performance V-8 or the big-block 390 V-8, the package would include a tachometer.

The smooth-shifting SelectShift Cruise-O-Matic transmission was a fully automatic unit and was available as an option in all Mustang models. This transmission also permitted manual shifting without a clutch, of course.

Suspension, Steering, and Brakes

Front Suspension

Ford Motor Company's literature in 1967 states: "The '67 Mustang front suspension is all-new and embodies many design improvements." All of the attaching points of the single lower arms and A-frame upper arms to the body were rubber bushings to help keep inherent friction to a minimum. The new lower arm was lengthened by 2½ inches and the upper A-frame arm pivot was lowered. Those changes provided more stability and a smoother ride. A special service feature was the incorporation of separate cam adjustments for both camber and caster, and it eliminated the adjustment shims that were previously used. The adjustments could be made faster, more accurately, and independent of one another.

The telescopic shock absorbers were mounted inside the coil springs and featured constant viscosity fluid to provide uniform damping of the suspension system under all climatic conditions.

The new lower control arm was connected to the chassis platform with a rubber-bushed control strut. Two large, sturdy bushings at the front of the strut permitted a slight controlled, horizontal wheel movement that helped the tires cushion small road irregularities, especially at high speeds. A rubber-bushed stabilizer bar provided effective sway control.

A unique option available on the Mustang was the heavy-duty suspension that included increased rate springs, larger recalibrated shock absorbers, and an increased diameter stabilizer bar. This option provided increased roadability and handling.

Rear Suspension

All Mustangs had wide, long rear springs in the Hotchkiss-type rear suspension. These four-leaf springs effectively cushioned bumps and road irregularities and absorbed the twisting action of the rear axle as it reacted to acceleration and braking forces. Special plastic liners at the spring tips reduced friction and helped absorb the smallest bumps.

A large, sturdy rubber bushing at the front mounting eye reduced road shock and noise and permitted slight horizontal wheel movement that helped absorb small irregularities. At the rear, the spring was held in a rubber-bushed, compression-type shackle to allow easy flexing on light impact and provide greater resistance to severe impact. Shock absorbers were angle-mounted to help reduce side sway to a minimum, and constant viscosity fluid was used for more uniform snubbing action in any weather.

When the optional heavy-duty suspension was installed, the rear suspension included heavy-duty springs and shock absorbers.

Steering

The Mustang's steering system in 1967 was a parallelogram linkage-type with a cross link and idler arm. The steering gear used was Ford's Magic-Circle recirculating ball-and-nut design. All new components were created to accommodate the new front suspension and increased tread width.

The ball joints were filled with polyethylene to provide lower friction characteristics and reduce the overall steering effort. The polyethylene

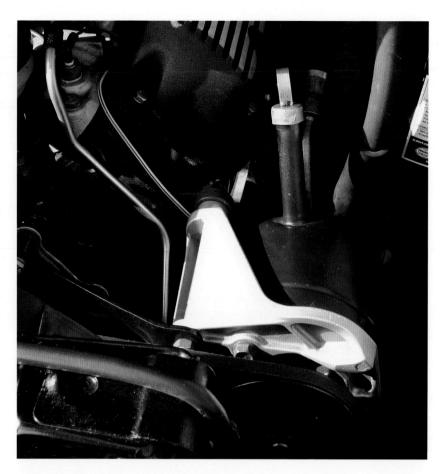

also provided better damping to help reduce shock feedback through the steering system.

The manual steering ratio was 25.3:1, compared to 27:1 from the 1966 model year, and offered faster and more responsive steering with less effort.

A faster ratio steering gear was used when either the optional competition handling package or optional power steering was selected. This gear provided an overall steering ratio of 20.3:1 and turned from lock to lock in 3.6 turns.

Brakes

All Mustangs for 1967 were equipped with a new dual hydraulic brake system. The standard brakes on all cars were a duo-servo design—self-energizing, single anchor, internal expanding, and air cooled. The linings were self-adjusting when the brakes were applied while the car was moving in reverse. Front wheel power disc brakes were optional on all V-8 powered Mustangs.

Heating and Ventilation

Ford went to great lengths in 1967 to assure its customers that much thought was given to a well-controlled heating, ventilation, and air conditioning system, as evidenced in Ford's literature: "A high capacity heater that can maintain comfortable passenger compartment temperatures

The power-steering pump and reservoir is shown here. Power steering was an option on all 1967 models.

Heater and air conditioner controls for 1967 were on the left lower side of the instrument panel on the driver's side. Air conditioning was an extra cost option.

Adjustable air registers, or vents, in the instrument panel allowed air to be directed to wherever was comfortable.

The factory Ford air conditioner was optional equipment on all Mustangs for 1967.

even in below zero weather is standard equipment on all Mustangs. The heater incorporates defroster ducts that direct a high volume of heated air through registers on either side of the radio speaker grille at the top of the instrument panel."

The thermostat used on all Mustang engines was 195 degrees Fahrenheit and provided faster warmup and extra heater capacity. The air for the heating system entered through the outside vent on top of the cowl. The temperature control was maintained by directing one part of the air through the heater core, while the other part was directed around it. The heated and unheated air was mixed together in the plenum chamber and directed out the defroster to defog the windshield. When extra defogging was required, all the heater output was directed through the defroster by moving the lever to "defrost." The blower was ordinarily used only to speed up the heat output or maintain the interior temperature at slow speeds. At moderate to fast road speeds, enough air was forced into the system to maintain comfortable passenger-compartment temperature.

There were two fresh air inlets on either side of the dashboard that could be opened to provide fresh air ventilation. The right vent was controlled by opening a door on the heater housing, and the left side inlet was controlled by a knob under the left side of the instrument panel. On the 2+2 fastback, a "Silent-Flo" ventilation system was used with the front air inlets and featured manually operated vents on the roof's rear quarters. The vents were designed to extract stale air and smoke, as well as defog the rear window. The vents could be fully opened with the windows closed to reduce wind noise and provide quiet air circulation. They also kept out the rain and dust. In cold weather, the vents could be partially opened to help circulate heated air to the rear compartment.

The SelectAire air conditioner was fully integrated into the instrument panel and heating system to provide year-round passenger comfort from one set of controls.

There were four air conditioning registers in the instrument panel: one at each end and two in the center. The registers were adjustable to distribute the air in the fashion most comfortable for the passengers. The unit had a three-speed blower and two air conditioning positions for further versatility and comfort.

REGULAR PRODUCTION OPTIONS

Engines

289-ci 200-horsepower V-8	105.63
289-ci 225-horsepower V-8	158.48
289-ci 271-horsepower V-8	
(with GT Equipment Group only)	433.55
390-ci 320-horsepower V-8	263.71

Transmissions

Cruise-O-Matic with 200 Six	188.18
Cruise-O-Matic with 200- or 225-horsepower V-8	197.89
Cruise-O-Matic with 271- or 320-horsepower V-8	220.17
Four-speed manual transmission with 200- or 225-horsepower	184.02
Four-speed manual transmission with all other V-8s	233.18
Heavy-duty three-speed manual transmission required with 320-horsepower V-8	79.20

Power Assists

Power convertible top	52.95
Power front disc brakes	64.77
Power steering	84.47

Comfort-Convenience Equipment

2+2 folding rear seat and access door	
(Sport Deck option)	64.77
Accent paint stripe	13.90
Center console (required radio)	50.41
Comfortweave vinyl trim (not available with convertible)	24.53
Competition Handling Package	
(with GT Equipment Group only)	388.53
Convenience control panel	39.50
Convertible safety glass rear window	32.44
Deluxe steering wheel	31.52
Exterior Decor Group	38.86
Fingertip speed control (required V-8 and Cruise-O-Matic)	71.30
Full-width front seat (not available with 2+2)	24.42
GT Equipment Group (with V-8s only)	205.05
Interior Decor Group (convertible)	94.36
Interior Decor Group (all others)	108.06
Limited-slip differential	41.60
Lower back panel grille	19.48
MagicAire heater (delete option)	31.52
Pushbutton radio AM	57.51
Pushbutton radio AM/FM	133.65
Rear deck luggage rack (2+2)	32.44
Remote-control outside mirror (standard on 2+2)	9.58
Rocker panel molding (standard on 2+2)	15.59
SelectAire air conditioner	356.09
Stereo-Sonic tape system (AM radio required)	128.49
Styled-steel wheels (2+2 only)	93.84
(All others)	115.11
Tilt-away steering wheel	59.93
Tinted windows and windshield	30.25
Two-tone paint (lower back grille)	12.95
Typical whitewall tire option	33.31
Vinyl-covered roof (hardtop)	74.36
Wide-oval sports tires (V-8 required)	62.35
Wheel covers (standard on 2+2)	21.34
Wire wheel covers (2+2)	58.24
Wire wheel covers (all others)	79.51

Wheels and Tires

All 1967 Mustangs were equipped with 14-inch steel wheels and 6.96x14 tires except the Mustangs equipped with the 390-ci V-8, which came with 7.35x14 tires.

Optional wheels were styled steel, wire wheel cover, and the latter with spinner. The 1967 styled steel version was wider than the 1966 version, due to the wider tire sizes available. There was also a bright trim ring included with this optional wheel.

The 14-inch wire-wheel covers were the same as the 1966 versions, except for the plain red center that replaced the blue spinners. The wire wheel cover with spinner was heavier than the unit previously listed and featured blue spinner centers that were recessed back toward the wheel cover, due to safety regulations.

OPPOSITE: The standard wheel cover for 1967 looks elegant with its wire wheel-like appearance. *Tom Shaw*

BELOW: This 1967 Shelby in Dark Moss Green is resplendent in the Colorado mountains. *Joyce Donaldson*

Shelby Mustangs

Body

Carroll Shelby's modifications to Mustang fastbacks were carried over for 1967. While the 1965 and 1966 Shelbys weren't radical departures from their stock brethren, it would be safe to say that the 1967–1970 Shelbys were. Starting with the 1967 model, the use of fiberglass parts was very liberal and drastically changed the Mustang's appearance.

The 1967 Shelby Mustang had a fiberglass nose section that replaced stock Mustang sheet metal. The front end of the car was extended by a whopping 3 inches! A custom grille housed a pair of 7-inch-diameter driving lights, and the stock Mustang front bumper was retained, minus the bumper guards. Other front section modifications included a fiberglass valance with large

cutout area for better cooling, and a fiberglass hood with an integrated hood scoop.

The sides of the car featured two scoops. One was attached to the quarter panel behind the door, and the other was attached to the C-pillar area. In most cases the lower scoop was functional and was used to cool the rear brakes. The upper scoops drew air out of the inside of the car.

Rocker panel graphics were standard on all 1967 Shelbys and featured either GT350 (289 Hi-Po) or GT500 (428-ci V-8) lettering. The Shelbys you see with wide LeMans stripes running over the top of the car had the striping done as a dealer-installed option.

The Shelby customized rear end featured 1967 Cougar taillights without the trim and a large rear ducktail-type spoiler. A racing style pop-open gas cap was used. The rear valance panel featured cutouts for 3-inch-diameter chrome exhaust tail pipes.

Interior
The 1967 Shelby Mustangs sported Interior Decor Groups. The speedometer is a 140-mile-per-hour unit, and the tach rolled all the way up to 8,000 rpm. A special underdash unit housed Stewart Warner oil pressure and amp gauges. The perforated three-spoke steering wheel rim was made from real wood and featured a round horn button with a special Shelby Cobra emblem. The fold-down rear seat was standard, along with a roll bar with inertia reel shoulder harnesses.

Engines
The Shelby GT350 sported a 289 K-code high-performance V-8. The horsepower rating was 306 (compared to a stock 289 engine's at 271), and the extra horses were derived from a high-rise Cobra aluminum intake manifold and a Holley 715-cfm unit (on four-speed models). Automatic Shelbys used a 595-cfm Autolite carburetor. The majority of 1967 Shelbys used the stock Ford oil pan, as opposed to the aluminum Cobra piece from 1966.

The GT500 Shelby packed a whopping 428-cube Ford engine (FE) rated at 355 horsepower. This motor featured a dual quad aluminum intake and two Holley 600-cfm carburetors.

The sleek lines of the 1967 Shelby GT500. *Tom Shaw*

OPPOSITE: The 428-cube FE—rated at 355 horsepower—was available in the Shelby GT500. *Tom Shaw*

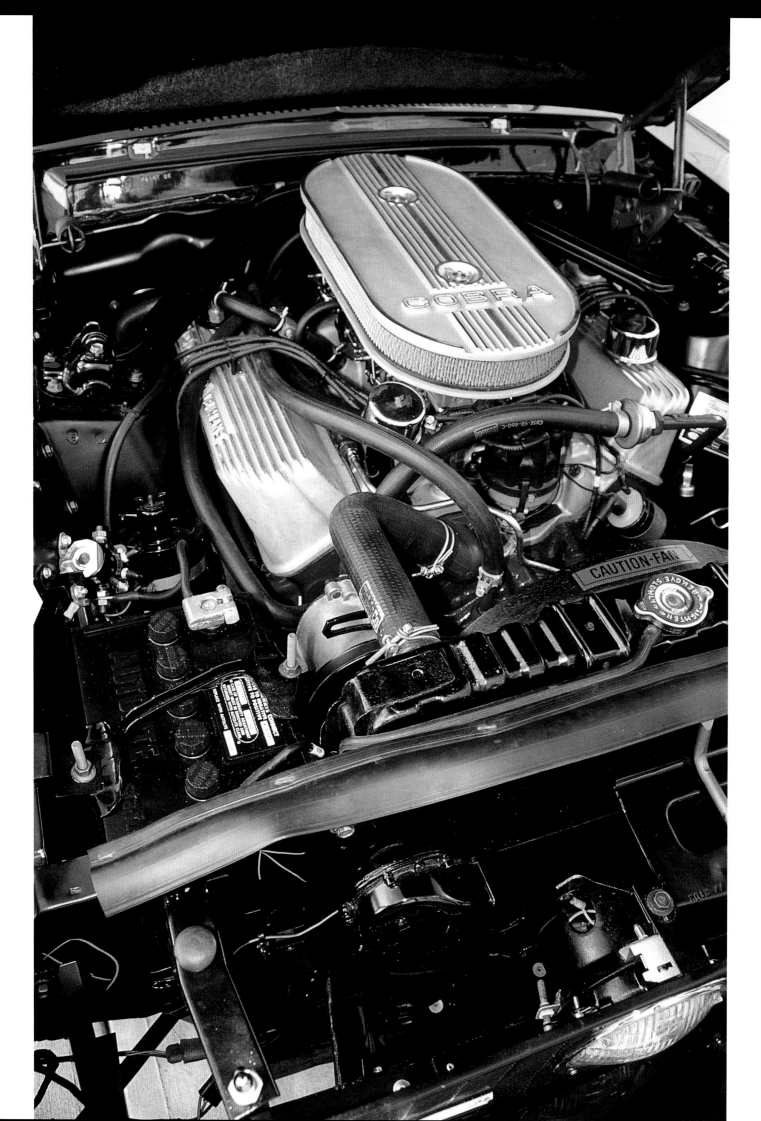

Chapter 3

1968

Ford saw that it had a huge hit in the new Mustang in 1965. The 1966 model continued on in the same tradition with very few changes. Why mess with success? That line of thinking paid off handsomely in 1966 as Mustang sales trumped the number of 1965 units sold and sent the growth charts into the stratosphere.

Since the 1967 Mustang had undergone such a drastic restyle and was very successful, Ford decided to keep changes to the 1968 car at a bare minimum. In fact, just like it was tough for the untrained eye to tell the difference between a 1965 and 1966 Mustang, the same held true of the 1967 and 1968 cars. Other than some minor

OPPOSITE & ABOVE: The eclectic Mustang GT/CS (California Special) appeared in 1968 as a regional model only. This car was aimed squarely at the Southern California market because Ford deemed it had the buyers to warrant it. The car featured: a blacked-out grille (notice the absence of the corral and pony); special Lucas fog lamps; Shelby-style fiberglass side scoops; Shelby-style rear quarter section with turned-up spoiler; Shelby taillights, special side and rear deck stripes; California Special emblems; and twist-type hood locks. Another specialty model, the High Country Special, basically mimicked the California Special and was sold as a special limited edition by Colorado Ford dealers. *Tom Shaw*

RIGHT: The full-color retail sales brochure for the 1968 Mustang was more dramatic than its 1967 counterpart.

trim differences, the most surefire sign distinguishing the two years was the addition of government-mandated side marker lights (reflectors on the rear) on the 1968 model. The simulated air scoops on the quarter panels were another difference that set the two years apart.

The year 1968 saw the continuation of the three body styles (hardtop, fastback, and convertible) and the addition of three more engines to the lineup: 302, 427, and 428. That model year also saw the deletion of the K- and A-code 289 powerplants. A couple of regional specialty models, the California Special and High Country Special, made the scene as one-year wonders.

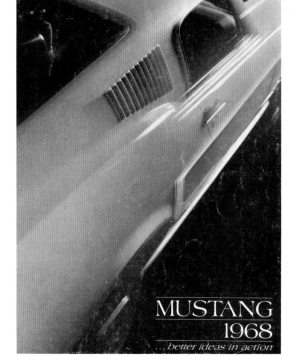

MUSTANG
1968
...*better ideas in action*

"Only Mustang Makes it Happen!" was the big theme for 1968. This full-page, full-color ad appeared in *Look* magazine in 1968.

OPPOSITE & BELOW: The Mustang hardtop for 1968 in Gulfstream Aqua (F). This car is equipped with the optional C-stripe and optional wheel covers.

Open up the rather understated "Mustang 1968 . . . better ideas in action" full-color brochure and get the full scoop on all the models: "Excitement. It starts here! It happens in a Mustang Hardtop. Why settle for an 'also ran' or second choice when the front runner, the original, can give you exactly what you're looking for?"

For the 1968 hardtop version, bucket front seats with all-vinyl upholstery were standard and individually adjustable for driver and passenger.

The five-dial instrument cluster in the fully padded instrument panel was the same as the previous year, as was the floor-mounted shift lever with any transmission. The indicator lights were built into the hood louvers, and Mustang's wide, bright rocker-panel molding added a sporty flair.

For performance, the hardtop was smooth and economical with a 200-ci, six-cylinder engine with self-adjusting valve lifters.

Some of the other Mustang features were reversible keys and the suspended accelerator pedal that adjusted to the driver's foot angle for extra comfort on long trips.

The glitzy brochure, this time packed with realistic photography, went on to tell the virtues of the Mustang 2+2: "Mustang 2+2 . . . a tempo that swings!"

The Silent-Flo Ventilation was standard and exclusive with Mustang 2+2. The options included the 2+2 folding rear seat with access door. When the seat was down, there was a convenient access door between the car and the trunk. The Convenience Group had a choice of three complete sound systems and included such features as a collapsible spare tire, rear window defogger, tinted glass, and remote-control outside rearview mirror.

The glamorous convertible had its own sporty verbiage: "Mustang Convertible . . . top up or down. It moves!"

The rest of the brochure went on about the wonders of the 1968 convertible and what it had to offer:

No question about it, a Mustang convertible is sure to open the door to a whole new, exciting world for you. Only Mustang makes it happen. It moves, and it moves people.

Of course, you get all of Mustang's standard features. But have you seen Mustang's optional convertible glass backlight? It's made of tempered glass . . . another of Ford's better ideas. You can clean it like the windshield. (No cloudiness, either.) It has another unique characteristic, one that's more than a conversation piece: it folds! The backlight actually folds across the center when the top is lowered. The two pieces are hinged with a translucent silicone rubber. This is just another reason why Mustang looks so neat and sleek when the top's down and the boot is in place.

Of course, there are a lot of other features you can select to make your Mustang convertible a one-of-a kind car. Sports tires, deluxe wheel covers, accent paint stripe, two-tone hood (for that extra sporty look), Interior Decor Group, Sports Trim Group, and a choice of four V-8 engines up to 390 cubic inches!

It's a pleasant task, designing your own Mustang.

Total 1968 Mustang production saw 317,423 units, of which 249,456 were hardtops, 42,582 were fastbacks, and 25,385 were convertibles. See table in Chapter 1 for complete individual model production listing.

Like the 1967 models, 1968 Mustangs featured Mustang script lettering and the tri-shield emblem with engine callouts on the lower fenders. The engine designator was for V-8-powered cars only.

Front side marker lights were government mandated for all 1968 model cars.

Rear side markers were also now required by law. In the 1968 Mustang's case, they were reflectors, not lights. This style was introduced on the 1968 cars, but the design changed after February 15, 1968.

This revised rear side marker reflector appeared on Mustangs after mid-February 1968.

The "pony" and "corral" were still up front and center on 1968 Mustangs, but the design was shallower than the 1967 versions.

Fog lamps were part of the package once again for the GT models.

The traditional Mustang side scoops were more subdued for 1968 with this simple piece of side trim.

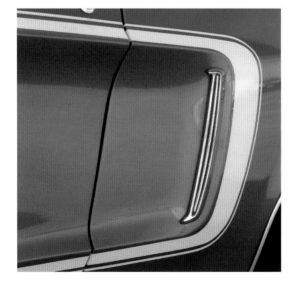

Mustang taillights were identical to the 1967 model. One single bulb illuminated all three bars. Turn signal and brake lights were integrated.

Body, Models, and Exterior Trim

Because the style was mostly a carryover from 1967, the word of the day for the 1968 Mustangs was refinement. Hardtop sales were down over the previous year, but this model continued to be the flagship Mustang model. The base price was set at $2,578.60; which was $117.04 more than the previous 1967 model.

The fastback carried a base price sticker of $2,689.26. If you can find a 1968 fastback today, you'll probably pay 10 times that for a car in need of a complete restoration. Good luck!

The convertible continued on with the glamour set and turned heads everywhere. The base price was $2,814.22, making it the most expensive model of the bunch.

Exterior Styling and Features

The 1968 Mustang continued its long hood, short deck, sports car styling with slight changes in sheet metal and new standard ornamentation.

- Bodyside panels had new simulated air scoop ornaments. The scoops combined with the sculptured side sheet metal to provide a feeling of motion and performance.
- New front sidelights and rear side reflectors contributed to safer nighttime driving.
- Full-length, bright metal rocker panel moldings were standard.
- Bright metal hubcaps with a Ford crest in the recessed center were standard on all models.
- The crisp mesh grille was deeply inset and featured an inner bright ring around the corralled Mustang.
- Single headlamps were set at either side of the grille. Parking lights and turn signals were recessed in the sheet metal below the full-width, wraparound front bumper.
- The new louvered hood had functional left and right turn-signal reminder lights set in louvers.
- The windshield, recessed rear window, and curved side windows were tastefully outlined with bright metal trim.
- The concave rear panel was framed by a bright molding and thin line bumper. Triple taillights/turn signals were set at either side of the rear panel. Back-up lights were mounted to the sheet metal below the rear bumper.
- On convertible models, the convertible top was five-ply vinyl and available in black or parchment. New hidden fasteners on the

1968 STANDARD EQUIPMENT

- Accelerator pedal: suspended type
- Alternator: 38 amps
- Armrests: front, energy absorbing
- Armrests: rear, ashtrays (convertible only)
- Ashtray: front
- Backup lights
- Battery: Sta-Ful design
- Body: rust resistant
- Brakes: self adjusting, dual system
- Bucket seats: foam padded, adjustable
- Carpets: 100 percent nylon, molded
- Choke: automatic
- Cigarette lighter
- Coat hooks
- Coolant: two years or 36,000 miles
- Courtesy lights: door switches
- Curved side glass
- Door checks: two stages
- Door hinges: bronze, bushed
- Door latches: bear-hug
- Door trim: all vinyl
- Emergency flashers
- Engine: 200 Six
- Exhaust emission control system (all engines)
- Finish: Super Diamond Lustre Enamel
- Front fenders: bolt-on
- Fuel tank: 17 gallons
- Glass: safety
- Glove box: instrument panel mounted
- Headlining: color-keyed vinyl (hardtop and fastback only)
- Heater and defroster: fresh air
- Hood latch: single action
- Hood louvers with turn-signal reminder lights
- Horns: dual
- Instrument panel: padded
- Insulated body
- Jack: scissors type, body side
- Lamps, bulbs: extended life
- Lubrication, chassis: 36,000 miles
- Maintenance: twice a year
- Mirror: inside rearview, day/night
- Mirror: outside rearview
- Molding: rear end
- Molding: rocker panel
- Muffler: aluminized and stainless steel
- Scuff plates: aluminum
- Seat belt: deluxe front and rear with reminder light
- Sun visors: padded, color-keyed
- Thermostat: 195 degrees Fahrenheit
- Transmission: three-speed manual
- Transmission lever: tunnel mounted
- Turn signals
- Upholstery: all vinyl
- Valve lifters: hydraulic
- Ventilation: Cowl-Aire intakes (hardtop and convertible only)
- Ventilation: Cowl-Aire plus roof vent outlets (fastback only)
- Windshield washers
- Windshield wipers: 15-inch electric, two speeds

The Mustang hardtop trunk was slight to say the least. At 9.2 cubic feet, however, it was the largest in the Mustang line. The convertible's trunk was 7.7 cubic feet, and the fastback measured in at a measly 5.1 cubic feet. But you didn't buy a Mustang to haul stuff around, now did you?

The louvered hood with integrated turn signals became a separate option in 1968.

The underside of the turn-signal hood shows the wiring layout.

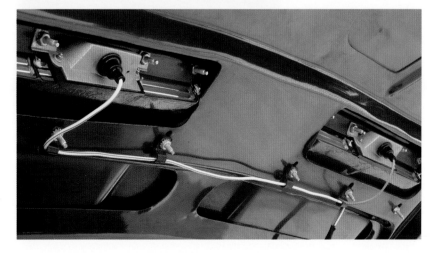

BODY SPECIFICATIONS

	Hardtop	Fastback	Convertible
Length (overall, inches)	183.6	183.6	183.6
Width (overall, inches)	70.9	70.9	70.9
Height (overall, inches)	51.6	51.6	51.6
Wheelbase (inches)	108	108	108
Curb weight (pounds)	2,696	2,723	2,856
(six cylinder, standard transmission)			

VIN/TRIM/DSO TAG DECODING FOR **1968**

Model Year Code
8= 1968

Assembly Plant Codes
F= Dearborn, Michigan
R= San Jose, California
T= Metuchen, New Jersey

Body Serial Codes
01= hardtop
02= fastback
03= convertible

Engine Codes
C= 289-ci eight-cylinder, 2 bbl
F= 302-ci eight-cylinder, 2 bbl
J= 302-ci eight-cylinder, 4 bbl
R= 428 cubic-inch eight cylinder, 4 bbl (Ram Air)
S= 390-ci eight-cylinder, 4 bbl
T= 200-ci six-cylinder, 1 bbl
W= 427-ci eight-cylinder, 4 bbl

Consecutive Number
The remaining six digits in the VIN indicate the vehicle's consecutive unit number assigned at the production line.

BODY STYLE CODES

63A= fastback standard (bucket seat)
63B= fastback Decor Group (bucket seat)
63C= fastback standard (bench seat)
63D= fastback Decor Group (bench seat)
65A= hardtop standard (bucket seat)
65B= hardtop Decor Group (bucket seat)
65C= hardtop standard (bench seat)
65D= hardtop Decor Group (bench seat)
76A= convertible standard (bucket seat)
76B= convertible Decor Group (bucket seat)
76C= convertible standard (bench seat)

COLOR CODES

6= Pebble Beige
B= Royal Maroon
F= Gulfstream Aqua
M= Wimbledon White
O= Sea Foam Green
R= Highland Green
U= Tahoe Turquoise
X= Presidential Blue

A= Raven Black
D= Acapulco Blue
I= Lime Gold
N= Diamond Blue
Q= Brittany Blue
T= Candyapple Red
W= Meadowlark Yellow
Y= Sunlit Gold

TRIM CODES

Standard Bucket Seats
2A= Black 2B= Blue 2D= Dark Red 2F= Saddle 2G= Ivy Gold 2K= Aqua
2U= Parchment 2Y=Nugget Gold

Interior Decor Group (Bucket Seats)
6A= Black 6B= Blue 6D= Dark Red 6F= Saddle 6G= Ivy Gold 6K= Aqua
6U= Parchment 6Y=Nugget Gold

TRIM CODES (CTD)

Bench Seat
8A= Black 8B= Blue 8D= Dark Red 8U= Parchment

Interior Decor Group (Bench Seat)
9A= Black 9B= Blue 9D= Dark Red 9U= Parchment

Bucket Seats (with Comfortweave Option)
7A= Black 7B= Blue 7D= Dark Red 7U= Parchment

Interior Decor Group (Buckets with Comfortweave Option)
5A= Black 5B= Blue 5D= Dark Red 5U= Parchment

DATE CODES

The number (1–31) appearing before the month letter indicates the day.

Month	First Year	Second Year
January	A	N
February	B	P
March	C	Q
April	D	R
May	E	S
June	F	T
July	G	U
August	H	V
September	J	W
October	K	X
November	L	Y
December	M	Z

DSO CODES

This code indicates the city/area in which the vehicle was originally destined for delivery.

11= Boston, Massachusetts	13= New York City, New York
15= Newark, New Jersey	16= Philadelphia, Pennsylvania
17= Washington, D.C.	21= Atlanta, Georgia
22= Charlotte, North Carolina	24= Jacksonville, Florida
25= Richmond, Virginia	27= Cincinnati, Ohio
28= Louisville, Kentucky	32= Cleveland, Ohio
33= Detroit, Michigan	34= Indianapolis, Indiana
35= Lansing, Michigan	37= Buffalo, New York
38= Pittsburgh, Pennsylvania	41= Chicago, Illinois
42= Fargo, North Dakota	43= Milwaukee, Wisconsin
44= Twin Cities, Minnesota	45= Davenport, Iowa
51= Denver, Colorado	52= Des Moines, Iowa
53= Kansas City, Missouri	54= Omaha, Nebraska
55= St. Louis, Missouri	61= Dallas, Texas
62= Houston, Texas	63= Memphis, Tennessee
64= New Orleans, Louisiana	65= Oklahoma City, Oklahoma
71= Los Angeles, California	72= San Jose, California
73= Salt Lake City, Utah	74= Seattle, Washington
75= Phoenix, Arizona	81= Ford of Canada
83= Government	84= Home Office Reserve
85= American Red Cross	89= Transportation Services
90–99= Export	

AXLE CODES

Conventional	Limited Slip	Axle Ratio
1		2.75
2		2.79
4		2.83
5	E	3.00
6	F	3.20
7	G	3.35
8	H	3.50
9		3.10

TRANSMISSION CODES

1= three-speed manual   5= four-speed manual
U= automatic (C6)   W= automatic (C4)

top boot added to the attractive top up or down appearance.

The GT Equipment Group ($146.71) could be ordered on any Mustang as long as it was equipped with a four-barrel V-8 engine. The GT Equipment Group for 1968 included GT ornamentation with the GT emblem mounted to the lower front fender. The letters "GT" were chromed to stand out against a black background. A special GT pop-open gas cap had the "G" stacked on top of the "T." The low restriction dual exhaust had chromed quad exhaust tips. Four-inch fog lights were set into the grille. GT "C" side stripes formed an extended letter "C" from the quarter panel forward to the leading edge of the front fenders. The package also featured GT chromed styled steel wheels, F70x14 wide oval white sidewall tires, heavy-duty suspension, and chrome engine components on 390- and 427-ci engines only.

The Sports Trim Group was available on all Mustang models and included woodgrain instrument panel appliqué, a two-tone painted hood, knitted vinyl inserts in the bucket seats for hardtop and fastback models, and bright wheel lip opening moldings. The V-8 models also received E70 wide oval white sidewall tires and argent-painted slotted wheels with bright trim rings.

The new-for-1968 Reflective Group included special reflective GT stripes and paint-on styled steel wheels. This package was only available on GT-equipped Mustangs.

Interior

Because the interior had been completely updated and restyled for the previous model year, changes to the 1968 Mustang's interior were minimal. At first glance, the interiors for the two years looked very similar. However, safety mandates forced a few revisions, and color choices were also updated.

1968 interior changes listed by Ford Motor Company:
- Vertically pleated, all-vinyl trims were available in eight decorator colors: Black, Blue, Red, Parchment, Aqua, Ivy Gold, Saddle, and Nugget Gold.
- Front door armrests were longer and wider for added comfort.
- Door handles were the convenient hinged paddle-type.
- Folding front seat backs automatically locked in upright position.

Interior Decor Group featured woodgrain appliqué on the instrument panel and steering wheel. This particular interior is from a California Special Mustang. *Tom Shaw*

The 1968 Mustang standard interior in Aqua (2K). Even the base interior looked very dressy with its darker seat inserts and door panels.

Chrome Mylar trim around darker-colored aqua door-panel inserts looks upscale in this base model.

- Horizontally pleated, all vinyl door panels were trimmed in bright Mylar.
- Durable 100 percent nylon carpeting was color-keyed to interior trim.
- Additional standard equipment features were foot-operated, dual-stream windshield washers; new color-keyed, two-spoke steering wheel; and an expanded safety package.

The 1968 instrument panel carried on with the Mustang's hooded theme. The gauge layout (two large pods and three smaller pods above) remained the same. The large pod on the left continued to house the speedometer (120 mile-per-hour), but the large pod on the right was different than the 1967 model. It housed the fuel gauge and alternator gauge for 1968. The three smaller pods contained upper left (upper left), clock (center; if so equipped), and temperature (right), with two rectangular slots between the three pods. While the slots on the 1967 model were for the windshield wipers and brake warning lights, on the 1968 model, the slots were for windshield wipers and seatbelt reminder/brake warning lights. Just like the 1967 model, the standard dash finish was in Camera Case black.

The Interior Decor Group ($123.86; $110.16 in Convertible) was available as an option again for 1968. It included:

- Woodgrain instrument panel inserts and woodgrain steering wheel with woodgrain appliqué in center section

The instrument panel showed two large pods containing a 120-mile-per-hour speedometer and fuel/alternator gauge. Note the white running horse symbol between the pods. This was illuminated when the high beams were turned on.

Camera case grain was standard trim on base models for 1968.

- Two-toned inner door panels with a top portion that included short horizontal pleats and a door pull; a horizontal woodgrain panel attached to the center of the panel; and a unique grille section with courtesy lights affixed to the bottom of the door
- Insert trim buttons on the seat backs
- Padded trim panels (hardtop only)
- A woodgrain roof console with twin reading lights and switches (not available on convertible)
- Vinyl grip on automatic transmission lever (Cruise-O-Matic only); woodgrain knob on manual transmissions
- Bright trim surrounds on the brake and clutch (if so equipped) pedals
- Padded trim panels (hardtop only)

Other interior options for 1968 had: rear window defogger (first year for Mustang and on hardtops and fastbacks only); full-width bench seat; seat belt for third passenger; speed control; Comfortweave vinyl trim (with knitted vinyl seat inserts); front shoulder harness; fold-down rear seat (in fastback model only); tachometer (8,000 rpm); SelectAire air conditioning; center console; convenience control panel; Courtesy Light Group; tilt steering wheel; deluxe steering wheel; AM radio; AM/FM stereo; AM/eight-track tape; front headrests; and an electric clock. For a complete listing of all options, see the options chart in this chapter.

Chassis

As described in Chapter 1, "the platform carries the body on the top, encloses the engine, and provides attaching points for the various chassis components. It also provides the basic structure

The push-button seatbelt was color-keyed to interior and featured pebble grain.

The remote-control driver's side mirror featured chrome bezel.

Full-width sill plates were made from stamped aluminum, featuring the Ford logo.

The 289-ci, C-code, two-barrel V-8 made its last stand for 1968. It was replaced by the 302 in 1969.

of the car. The platform is made up of a box-section front and rear side rails tied in securely to heavy boxed-in rocker panels. These components are connected by five heavy-gauge crossmembers to form an extrastrong ladder-type framing under the car. The front and rear side rails extend partially under, and are welded to, the floor pan. The full-depth, full-length tunnel down the center of the floor pan adds a backbone to give the structure maximum rigidity. The full-depth side panels in the engine compartment are welded to the front side rails at the bottom and to the cowl at the rear. The tops of these panels are pressed over

to form a wide flange and increase front end rigidity. A one-piece stamping with a deep channel section at the top connects the inside panels across the front."

Regardless of the car's engine size, all Mustangs were based on the same platform chassis. Upgraded suspension components compensated for the weight differences in engines.

Engines

200-ci Six

Ford's 200-ci six-cylinder engine was standard on all Mustang models for 1968. Ford states that "refinements for 1968 include a dual inlet air cleaner that draws in air warmed by the exhaust manifold, or cooler air from under the hood, or a combination of both. This provides faster

BASE EQUIPMENT ENGINE: T-CODE

- Bore and stroke: 3.68x3.13
- Carburetor: Autolite 1100, 1V
- Compression ratio: 8.8:1
- Displacement: 200 ci
- Horsepower: 115 at 3,800 rpm
- Torque: 190 ft-lbs at 2,200 rpm
- Type: inline six-cylinder, overhead valve
- Valve lifters: hydraulic

warmup, reduces carburetor icing, and helps contribute to lower exhaust emissions.

"The seven main bearing crankshaft, an outstanding feature of this engine, is retained for 1968. The use of seven main bearings provides for extra smooth operation and greater durability."

Quick facts:

- Seven main bearings: smoother engine operation, less vibration, longer engine life
- Hydraulic valve lifters: quiet operation, low maintenance
- Large valves: more efficient breathing, more seat area for better cooling and less burning
- Short stroke design: less vibration, less wear
- Single-venturi carburetor: economical operation
- Six-month or 6,000-mile oil filter: reduced maintenance, improved oil filtering
- Automatic choke: senses ambient and coolant temperatures, helps prevent flooding on semiwarm starts
- Compression ratio of 8.8:1: better efficiency on regular or economy gasoline
- Thin wall casting: better cooling, less weight
- Precision-molded crankshaft: dependable, smooth operation

- Weather-insulated ignition system: reliable starts under all climatic conditions

289-ci V-8 2V

The two-barrel Challenger V-8 was the base V-8 engine for Mustang, and as Ford described in 1968: "Refinements introduced over years of production have made this the most popular Ford V-8 engine. The efficient valve train improves reliability and durability while cutting maintenance intervals. Rocker arms are guided by the valves themselves, thus cutting down on close tolerances. Low inertia valve springs aid performance while cutting down on wear. Overall performance has been improved by a new two-venturi carburetor. The 289 2V is a lightweight,

The 302-ci, J-code, four-barrel V-8 was rated at 235 horsepower at 4,800 rpm. *Tom Shaw*

OPTIONAL EQUIPMENT ENGINE:
C-CODE (CHALLENGER)

- Bore and stroke: 4.00x2.87
- Carburetor: Autolite 2100 (280 cfm), 2V
- Compression ratio: 8.7:1
- Displacement: 289 ci
- Horsepower: 195 at 4,600 rpm
- Torque: 288 ft-lbs at 2,600 rpm
- Type: eight cylinder, overhead valve
- Valve lifters: hydraulic

powerful, and quiet engine that ideally suits the requirements of the buyer who wants excellent economy of operation."

Quick facts:

- Lightweight cast-iron construction: used advanced, thin wall casting techniques
- Short stroke design: less friction, longer engine life
- Full-length, full-circle water jackets: uniform cylinder temperature with a minimum of hot spots
- Autothermic piston design: maintained critical clearances required for smooth efficiency
- Hydraulic valve lifters: no adjustment required
- Automatic choke: sensed ambient and coolant temperatures; helped prevent flooding on semiwarm starts
- Two-venturi carburetor: newly designed for improved economy and performance
- High-capacity fuel filter: inline design to provide maximum filtration
- Six-month or 6,000-mile oil filter: reduced maintenance, improved oil filtering
- Autolite power tip spark plugs: self-cleaning, extra long firing tip
- Dual advance distributor: correct spark advance for all driving conditions

302-ci V-8 2V and 4V

Mustang's new-for-1968 V-8 engine, the 302-ci V-8, was staged to replace the 289. Ford described the new 302 as having "many of the fine features found in the performance proven 289 V-8. For its cubic-inch displacement, the 302 V-8 has an extremely compact package size and is lightweight. Features include specially designed high efficiency combustion chambers, dual inlet air

cleaner system, extra strong short connecting rods and deep skirt pistons." For 1968 only, the J-code, four-barrel version was a viable optional upgrade from the two-barrel, F-code version.

Quick facts:

- Molded crankshaft: extra engine stability, smoother operation
- Connecting rods and pistons: short connecting rods with extrastrength design, deep skirt pistons with tolerance for longer engine wear
- Hot and cold dual inlet cleaner system: reduced throttle plate icing in cold weather, improved engine operation required for emission control
- Full-length, full-circle water jackets: uniform cylinder temperature with a minimum of hot spots
- High capacity fuel filter: inline design to provide maximum filtration
- Hydraulic valve lifters: no adjustment required
- Dual advance distributor: correct spark advance for all driving conditions
- Six-month or 6,000-mile oil filter: reduced maintenance, improved oil filtering
- Lightweight cast-iron construction: advanced thin wall castings

390-ci V-8 4V

In 1968, Ford introduced a hot and cold dual inlet air cleaner to help regulate the intake air temperature. This air cleaner helped reduce carburetor icing, speed warmup, and contribute to lower exhaust emission. The GT version gained extra power from the special carburetor, camshaft, and ignition components.

Quick facts:

- Chrome dress-up kit: standard on the 325 horsepower version; included chrome-plated air cleaner, valve covers, oil filter, dip stick, and radiator cap
- Full-flow fuel filter: inline design to provide maximum filtration
- High-performance valve springs and damper assembly: greater resistance to fatigue and wear
- Six-month or 6,000-mile oil filter: reduced maintenance, improved oil filtering

---

OPTIONAL EQUIPMENT ENGINE: F-CODE

- Bore and stroke: 4.00x3.00
- Carburetor: Ford 2100 (290 cfm), 2V
- Compression ratio: 9.5:1
- Displacement: 302 ci
- Horsepower: 220 at 4,400 rpm
- Torque: 300 ft-lbs at 2,600 rpm
- Type: eight cylinder, overhead valve
- Valve lifters: hydraulic

OPTIONAL EQUIPMENT ENGINE: J-CODE (1968 ONLY)

- Bore and stroke: 4.00x3.00
- Carburetor: Autolite 4300 (470 cfm) 4V
- Compression ratio: 10.5:1
- Displacement: 302 ci
- Horsepower: 235 at 4,800 rpm
- Torque: 318 ft-lbs at 3,200 rpm
- Type: eight cylinder, overhead valve
- Valve lifters: hydraulic

OPTIONAL EQUIPMENT ENGINE: S-CODE (GT)

- Bore and stroke: 4.05x3.78
- Carburetor: Holley 4150 (600 cfm), 4V
- Compression ratio: 10.5:1
- Displacement: 390 ci
- Horsepower: 325 at 4,800 rpm
- Torque: 427 ft-lbs at 3,200 rpm
- Type: eight cylinder, overhead valve
- Valve lifters: hydraulic

- 10.5:1 compression ratio: maximum power from premium fuels
- Camshaft lobe profile: more usable torque with a smooth idle
- Dual advance distributor: correct spark advance for all driving conditions
- Lightweight, cast-iron construction: advanced thin wall casting techniques
- Alternate valve spacing: higher volumetric efficiency, elimination of hot spots in cylinder block and heads
- Free-flow exhaust system: large exhaust passages, individual exhaust header to minimize exhaust pressure, twin pipes and mufflers
- Short stroke design: less friction, longer engine life
- Low-capacity oil sump: four-quart design, better circulation and cooling

427-ci V-8 4V

There was indeed a 427 that made its way into a Mustang. For the first part of the 1968 model year, Ford stuffed the legendary 427 FE into its pony car. FoMoCo's ad verbiage said it all: "The 427 V-8 is a true high-performance engine offering the ultimate in power and performance with outstanding reliability for sustained high rpm operation."

The addition of hydraulic valve lifters was new for 1968 and offered extra-quiet operation and eliminated periodic valve adjustment. The 427 was offered only with a heavy-duty version of Ford's SelectShift Cruise-O-Matic. All cars equipped with this engine feature had many special heavy-duty components such as a fan, radiator, front and rear suspension, driveshaft, and rear axle differential.

Quick facts:
- Compression ratio of 10.9:1: high-compression cylinder heads obtained maximum power from premium fuel
- Aluminum intake manifold: large, unobstructed intake passages
- Large intake and exhaust valves: free breathing, high volumetric efficiency
- Special high-rpm camshaft: delivered maximum power at high rpm
- Heavy-duty valve springs: with hydraulic valve lifters they helped eliminate valve float at high rpm
- Impact extruded pistons: designed for superior resistance to heat and stress, coupled with special connecting rods designed to withstand very high loads
- Cross-bolted main bearing caps: contained high-speed inertia loading
- High-capacity oil pump: high-pressure lubrication at all speeds
- High-volume fuel pump: coupled with inline fuel filter for maximum fuel supply under all operating conditions
- Free-flow exhaust: special exhaust headers with large exhaust passages; more efficient scavenging of exhaust gases, twin pipes, and dual mufflers
- Chrome dress-up kit: chrome-plated air cleaner, valve covers, oil filler, dip stick, radiator cap

428-ci V-8 4V

The vaunted 428 Cobra Jet engine made its way into Mustang as a midyear intro and prompted *Hot Rod* magazine to state in its March 1968 issue, "The Cobra Jet will be the utter delight of every Ford lover and the bane of all the rest because, quite frankly, it is the fastest running Pure Stock in the history of man." The 428 was the largest FE engine ever built, and Ford had a field day with it in the 1968 Mustang. The car's light weight and the engine's vastly underrated horsepower (in reality, it had over 400 horsepower) proved to be a terror at the drag strip. *Hot Rod* magazine tests pegged it at 13.56 seconds at 106.64 miles per hour in the quarter-mile.

Quick facts:
- Full-length, full-circle water jackets: designed to take advantage of thin wall casting, permitted higher overall engine operating temperature for increased performance capabilities
- New exhaust header-type manifolds: larger inside dimensions and extended runner lengths blended into a larger collection chamber to aid in the extraction of exhaust gases—especially in the high rpm capabilities of the 428s

---

OPTIONAL EQUIPMENT ENGINE: W-CODE (EARLY 1968 ONLY)

- Bore and stroke: 4.23x3.78
- Carburetor: Holley 4150 (780 cfm), 4V
- Compression ratio: 10.9:1
- Displacement: 427 ci
- Horsepower: 390 at 5,600 rpm
- Torque: 460 ft-lbs at 3,200 rpm
- Type: eight cylinder, overhead valve
- Valve lifters: hydraulic

OPTIONAL EQUIPMENT ENGINE: R-CODE (RAM AIR, MIDYEAR INTRO)

- Bore and stroke: 4.13x3.98
- Carburetor: Holley 4150 (735 cfm), 4V
- Compression ratio: 10.6:1
- Displacement: 428 ci
- Horsepower: 335 at 5,600 rpm
- Torque: 445 ft-lbs at 3,400 rpm
- Type: eight cylinder, overhead valve
- Valve lifters: hydraulic

- Electronically balanced crankshaft: a vibration damper, floated and mounted on rubber, on the front end of the crankshaft counteracted torsional vibration and provided smoother operation.
- Heavy-duty valve springs: allowed engine to exceed 5,000 rpm without encountering valve float
- Special high lift camshaft: stepped bearings reduced any possibility of damage during assembly; cam lobes were precision ground to provide maximum power at high rpm
- Dual advance distributor: correct spark advance was maintained for all driving conditions; centrifugal advance plus vacuum-controlled advance permit more precise distributor calibration for smoother, more efficient engine operation
- Full-flow fuel filter: maximum filtration was provided with minimum restriction for higher efficiency and power output

The Ram Air–equipped 428 used an air cleaner assembly with a vacuum-actuated bypass inlet valve mounted in the top. When the engine was operated at nearly full throttle, the vacuum motor would open the large air cleaner bypass valve and allow the additional air to flow directly into the air cleaner assembly.

Transmissions

For 1968, the base transmission was the three-speed manual. This was a fully synchronized transmission that was standard with the 200-ci six-cylinder, the 289 2V, and 302 2V engines. The 390-ci V-8 required a heavy-duty version of this transmission at extra cost.

A four-speed manual transmission was optional with all engines except the 200-ci six-cylinder and the optional 427-ci V-8. Ford described the transmission as "fully synchronized in all forward gears, permitting upshifts and downshifts at reasonable car speeds without gear clash or noise."

The smooth-shifting SelectShift Cruise-O-Matic transmission was a fully automatic unit available as optional equipment in all Mustang models. The C6 heavy-duty version of this transmission was standard with the 427-ci V-8. This transmission also permitted manual shifting.

Suspension, Steering, and Brakes

Front Suspension

Suspension on the 1968 Mustangs was improved again, as stated in FoMoCo's sales brochure: "The Mustang ball joint front suspension has improved ride characteristics because of the substitution of a new, curved 'hockey stick' lower arm strut. Incorporating a softer front rubber bushing, this strut allows front wheels to move back more easily under impact helping the tires cushion slight road irregularities. In addition, new precompressed strut insulator bushings provide improved caster alignment, giving better steering and handling."

All of the attaching points on the body, along with the single lower arms and A-frame upper arms in the front suspension, had rubber bushings to minimize friction. The separate cam adjustments for both camber and caster was a service feature that eliminated adjustment shims so adjustments could be made faster, more accurately, and independent of each other.

The long coil springs mounted on top of the upper suspension arms provided a long vertical wheel travel that absorbed bumps without bottoming out. Shocks were mounted vertically inside the coil springs. A new fluid was introduced in 1968 that had more constant viscosity, was used in the telescopic shock absorbers, and provided optimum control under all climatic conditions.

The heavy-duty suspension that included increased rate springs, larger and recalibrated shock absorbers, and an increased diameter stabilizer bar was also available and provided better handling.

Rear Suspension

All Mustangs employed wide, long rear springs in the Hotchkiss-type rear suspension. The four leaf springs cushioned bumps and road irregularities and absorbed the twisting action of the rear axle as it reacted to acceleration and braking. Special plastic liners were used at the spring tips to reduce friction and absorb the smallest bumps.

The SelectShift Cruise-O-Matic transmission was fully automatic and was available as optional equipment in all Mustang models. This was how it appeared without the optional center console.

A large, resilient rubber bushing at the front mounting eye reduced road shock and noise. It also permitted slight horizontal wheel movement that helped absorb small movements. The rear spring was held in a compression-type shackle with a rubber bushing, which allowed it to flex easily on light impact, and provided greater resistance to severe impact. Shock absorbers were angle-mounted to reduce side sway to a minimum, and constant-viscosity fluid was used for more uniform snubbing action in any weather. When the optional heavy-duty suspension was installed, the rear suspension included heavy-duty springs and shock absorbers.

Steering

The Mustang's steering system was described by Ford in 1968 literature: "A parallelogram, linkage type steering system with a cross link and idler arm is used on all 1968 Mustangs. The steering gear used is Ford's Magic-Circle recirculating ball-and-nut type."

The ball joint sockets were filled with polyethylene and provided lower friction characteristics and reduced overall steering effort. The polyethylene also helped reduce shock feedback through the steering system.

The manual steering ratio was 25.3:1. A faster ratio steering gear of 20.3:1 was used when the optional competition handling package or optional power steering was installed. The gear turned from lock to lock in 3.6 turns.

Brakes

The 1968 Mustangs were equipped with a dual hydraulic brake system. The standard brakes on all cars were a duo-servo design—self-energizing, single anchor, internal expanding, and air cooled. The linings were self-adjusting when the brakes were applied while the car moved in reverse. Front wheel power disc brakes were optional on all V-8-powered Mustangs.

Heating and Ventilation

Although the design of the heater control panel changed slightly for the 1968 model year, the operating system was identical to the 1967 model.

The 195-degree Fahrenheit thermostat used on all Mustang engines provided faster warmup and extra heater capacity. The air for the heating system entered through the outside vent on top of the cowl, and the temperature control was maintained by directing one part of the air through the heater core and the other part of air around it. The heated and unheated air was mixed together in the plenum chamber and directed out the defroster to defog the windshield. When extra defogging was required, all the heater

Front power disc brakes were optional on all models for 1968.

output went through the defroster when the lever was moved to "defrost." The blower was ordinarily used only to speed up the heat output or maintain the interior temperature in slow moving traffic. Sufficient air was forced into the system at moderate to fast road speeds to maintain comfortable passenger compartment temperature.

BELOW: Similar in design to the 1967 model, the heater and air conditioner controls were designed as one unit.

BOTTOM: The heater is visible from under the bottom of the instrument panel on the passenger side.

Wheels and Tires

The standard 1968 Mustang wheel was a 14x5-inch stamped steel unit with vent holes. Mustangs equipped with the base six-cylinder engine utilized wheels with a four-lug bolt pattern. Like the previous model year, the standard tire was 6.96x14. Mustangs equipped with the 390-ci V-8 came with 14x6 wheels and 7.35x14 tires. The base wheel cover was a 10½-inch hubcap.

Optional wheels included the styled steel, wheel cover, deluxe wheel cover, and a wire wheel cover. For 1968, the styled steel wheel was a slotted-type piece available either in painted argent or chrome with a chrome-trim ring and hubcap.

The 14-inch wheel cover featured short, bright spokes with rectangular slots. The areas between the spokes were dark gray. The deluxe wheel cover was similar to the regular wheel cover but included a red center with a Mustang emblem. The wire wheel cover featured bright spokes and a red center with a Mustang emblem.

Mustangs were equipped with a 195-degree Fahrenheit thermostat that was used on all engines.

BELOW: The 14-inch steel wheels with five lugs were standard on Mustangs with eight-cylinder engines. Six-cylinder cars used four-lug 14-inch wheels.

BELOW RIGHT: The optional radial spoke wheel cover graced most Mustangs in 1968.

Two fresh air inlets, one each side of the dashboard, could be opened to provide fresh air ventilation. The right side vent was controlled by opening a door on the heater housing; a knob under the left side of the instrument panel controlled the left side inlet. On the 2+2 fastback, a Silent-Flo ventilation system was used with the front air inlets and featured manually operated vents on the roof's rear quarters. Designed to draw out stale air and defog the rear window, the vents could be opened with the windows closed to reduce wind noise and provide quiet air circulation throughout the passenger compartment. In cold weather, the vents could be partially opened to circulate heated air to the rear compartment. The SelectAire air conditioner was an option for 1968 with a manufacturer's suggested retail price (MSRP) of $360.30.

Shelby Mustangs

In 1968 Carroll Shelby moved his production facilities from Los Angeles to Livonia, Michigan, for two reasons: his lease was going to expire at the California plant and there was a lack of high-quality fiberglass in the Los Angeles area.

For 1968, Carroll introduced the Cobra name into his cars. Shelby Mustangs were now known as the Shelby Cobra GT350 or GT500.

The 1967 Mustang had gone through such a radical departure from the 1966 versions, so there

REGULAR PRODUCTION OPTIONS

Engines
289-ci 195-horsepower V-8	105.63
302-ci 230-horsepower V-8	171.77
390-ci 325-horsepower V-8	263.71

Transmissions
Four-speed manual transmission (with 195-horsepower and 230-horsepower V-8s)	184.02
Four-speed manual transmission (with 325-horsepower V-8)	233.18
SelectShift Cruise-O-Matic (with Six)	191.12
SelectShift Cruise-O-Matic (with 195-horsepower and 230-horsepower V-8s)	200.85
SelectShift Cruise-O-Matic (with 325-horsepower V-8)	233.17

Power Assists
Power convertible top	52.95
Power front disc brakes (V-8s only: required with 325-horsepower V-8 on GT Equipment Group)	64.77
Power steering	84.47

Comfort-Convenience Equipment
Accent paint stripe	13.90
AM/FM stereo radio	181.39
Center console (radio required)	53.71
Convenience Group (console required with SelectAire)	32.44
Convertible glass backlight	38.86
Deluxe wheel covers (not available with GT Group or V-8 Sports Trim Group)	34.33
GT Equipment Group (with 230-horsepower or 325-horsepower V-8 with power disc brakes; not available Sports Trim Group or optional wheel covers)	146.71
Fingertip speed control (with V-8 and SelectShift)	73.83
Full-width front seat (hardtop and 2+2; not available with console)	32.44
Remote-control outside mirror (left-hand side)	9.58
Interior Decor Group (convertible; models with full-width front seat)	110.16
Interior Decor Group (all others without full-width front seat)	123.86
Limited-slip differential (V-8s only)	41.60
Pushbutton radio (AM)	61.40
SelectAire air conditioner	360.30
Sport deck rear seat (2+2 only)	64.77
Stereo-Sonic tape system (AM radio required)	133.86
Tilt-away steering wheel	66.14
Tilt-away steering wheel	66.14
Tinted windows and windshield	30.25
Two-tone hood paint	19.48
Vinyl-covered roof (hardtop only)	74.36
Wheel covers (not available with GT Group or V-8 Sports Trim Group)	21.34
Whitewall tire option	33.31
Wide-oval tire option (with V-8 only)	78.53

OPPOSITE: The 1968 Shelby Cobra GT350 in Diamond Blue. *Doug Bennett*

OPPOSITE BELOW: The Cobra Jet version of the 428 was standard in the GT500KR. *Tom Shaw*

was no need for Ford to change for 1968. The same basically held true for the Shelby cars. The biggest changes occurred at the front of the car and included a new front nose piece and a sleek new dual scoop fiberglass hood.

The biggest news was the addition of two new models to the lineup for 1968. The convertible model was available as a GT350 or GT500. The GT500KR (King of the Road) was introduced midyear and coincided with Ford's introduction of the 428 Cobra Jet engine.

The sides of the car featured two scoops like the pieces used in 1967: one was attached to the quarter panel just behind the door, and the other

The King of the Road: Shelby Cobra GT500KR convertible. *Tom Shaw*

was attached to the C-pillar area. Side marker lights (reflectors on the rear panels) were a government-mandated safety item. Rocker panel graphics were the same as the 1967 Shelbys and featured GT350, GT500, or GT500KR lettering.

The Shelby customized rear end featured 1965 Thunderbird taillights and a large rear ducktail spoiler. A racing-style pop-open gas cap was used. The rear valance panel was from the standard Mustang GT and had exhaust cutouts. Chrome exhaust tips were the large diameter "pipe inside a pipe" type on GT350 and GT500s, but the later model GT500KRs utilized the GT quad exhaust tips.

Interior

The 1968 Shelby Cobras sported Interior Decor Groups. A center console was now a standard item, but it was nothing like the unit used in stock Mustangs. The new Shelby console featured a pair of Stewart Warner gauges (oil and amps) that were mounted side-by-side in the center of the console underneath the radio. The fold-down rear seat, roll bar, and inertia reel seat belts were standard like the 1967 models.

Engines

The Shelby Cobra GT350 utilized the 302 four-barrel V-8 rated at 250 horsepower. The engine was modified with a Cobra aluminum intake and a 600-cfm Holley carb.

The Shelby Cobra GT500s were powered by a 360-horsepower version of the 428 Ford Police Interceptor engine. A Cobra aluminum intake with a 715-cfm Holley was standard.

The Shelby Cobra GT500KR received the Cobra Jet version of the 428. The engine was introduced midyear; it replaced the GT500.

ABOVE: The Shelby GT 500 fastback in Candy Apple Red.

LEFT: Hood louvers were molded into the special Shelby fiberglass hood.

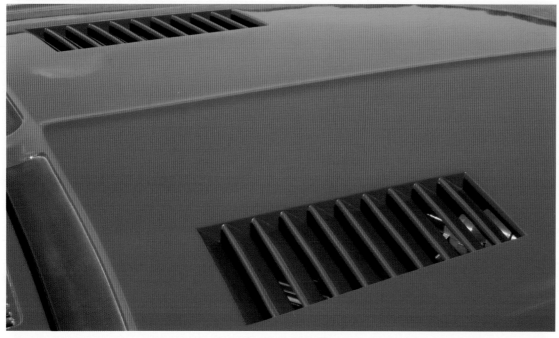

ABOVE: All Shelbys, from day one, received their own VIN tags at Shelby's factory.
LEFT: The GT500KR says it all: "King of the Road."

The 1965 Thunderbird taillights were used on 1968 Shelbys. Sequential turn signals added to the Shelby's striking good looks.

Roll bars played a huge part in the Shelby's interior, as evidenced by this photo.

The 1968 Shelbys sported the top of the line interiors. The Interior Decor Group added to the car's luxury side.

Shelby's optional 15-inch, 10-spoke aluminum wheels were unique and probably the toughest looking wheels of the day.

Chapter 4

1969

The year 1969 saw a huge and dramatic restyling exercise. The three body styles continued on in hardtop, fastback, and convertible form, although the terms "fastback" and "2+2" were now a thing of the past; "SportsRoof" was now the correct nomenclature. Memories of Arte Johnson from *Rowan & Martin's Laugh-In* as he ran his hand down the Mustang's sloping back glass and up over the new built-in spoiler comes to mind.

The all-new-for-1969 Mustangs still rode on a 108-inch wheelbase, but they were now 1 inch wider, 1 inch lower, and almost 4 inches longer than the 1967–1968 cars. The way of the future was becoming evident; big cars (even big pony cars) were right around the corner.

OPPOSITE & ABOVE:
This base Mustang
hardtop for 1969 is
equipped with a 428 SCJ
and styled steel wheels.

RIGHT: The retail sales
brochure for 1969 was
very dramatic. What
could be bolder than
someone driving right
toward you in a new
Mach 1?

A lot of folks refer to the 1969 model year as
the year that Mustang went from pony car to muscle car. This is understandable given the car's
growing dimensions and ever-increasing range of
high-performance powerplants. In addition to the
302, 390, and 428 engines, there were three more
RPO engines: the 351, a non–Ram Air 428, and
an upgraded 250-ci six-cylinder motor. If you
wanted something more out of the ordinary, you
could order up a Boss 302 or the NASCAR-spec
Boss 429. In all, there were 10 available
engine/package options for 1969.

Some specialty body-style/trim/performance
packages were introduced in 1969: the Mach 1
and the Grandé. The GT Equipment Group was
still an option, but it was overshadowed by the
Mach and Boss cars.

The retail sales brochure for 1969 played up the
Mach 1 and Grandé to the hilt. The Boss 302 and
Boss 429 had their own sales literature. The slogan
for the year was: "Mustang Mach 1 . . . new power
play." There were five new Mustangs for 1969. The

SportsRoof with a sporty rear deck spoiler, ventless side glass, new grille, and quad headlamps were latest additions to the 1969 Mustang.

With the new Mach 1, five V-8 engines were offered—two new 351s (a two- or four-barrel carb), each of which had a simulated scoop, and the virile 428 4V Cobra Jet Ram Air with hood air scoop. The Mach 1 was outfitted with GT-type equipment, such as dual exhausts with the four larger engines; wide-oval belted white sidewall tires on steel wheels; competition shocks, springs, and stabilizer bar; foam-padded, vinyl-trimmed high-back buckets; racing mirrors; woodlike, three-spoke rim-blow steering wheel; clock; console; teak-toned highlight on the dash, door panels, and console; bright floor pedal pads; low-gloss paint on the hood and cowl; pin-type hood lock latches; and reflective stripes.

The fully synchronized three-speed manual was standard with either 351 engine. The four-speed manual or SelectShift was available with all engines. A tachometer was added with the four-speed when either of the 428 engines or the 390 was ordered. The tachometer could also be ordered separately with any engine and transmission.

In stark contrast, the pages of the brochure went on about the new luxury Mustang. "Mustang Grandé . . . your first Mustang made life more delicious, right? So how about a second helping?

"Sheer luxury. All planned to reflect your lavish mood. As you can see from its very handsome styling and attractive appointments, such as wire-style wheel covers, dual racing-style mirrors, and neat two-tone narrow tape stripes. Grandé says here is the elegant Mustang."

The Grandé had a standard 200-ci, seven-main-bearing, six-cylinder engine. The brand-new 4.1-liter six-cylinder, the 302-ci V-8, or one of other five V-8s, one of which went all the way up to 335 horsepower, were the Grandé's engine options. The three-speed manual shift was standard, but the SelectShift transmission was an option.

Ford really turned up the heat with model and engine availability for the 1969 model year, and tried to stay a jump ahead of the competition because the 1969 Camaro was stealing away sales. GM tallied total Camaro sales that year at 243,095 units, which was just 56,000 units less than Mustang.

ABOVE & OPPOSITE: The Candyapple Red paint of this amazing 1969 Mach 1 is literally glowing under rare stormy Southern California skies. The owner added sport slats and a chin spoiler.

All-new-for-1969 taillights carried on the traditional three-bar theme.

The hardtop and convertible now sported a reverse-facing side scoop accented with chrome trim.

Total 1969 Mustang production was 299,036 units, of which 150,637 were hardtops; 133,801 were fastbacks; and 14,598 were convertibles. See table in Chapter 1 for complete individual model production listing.

Body, Models, and Exterior Trim

For the most part, everything changes when a Mustang is completely repenned. The completely new-for-1969 styling affected each of three body styles.

The hardtop, the Mustang line's perennial best seller, enjoyed sales of 150,637 units, but that was down considerably, almost 100,000 units, from the 1968 model year. The base price was $2,618, which was the same base price of the SportsRoof.

The sharp new base convertible was now priced at $2,832, which was $17.78 more than the previous 1968 ragtops. The Mach 1, with its base 351 2V powerplant, went for a healthy $3,122, but considering the goodies that were included, it was a steal.

The luxo Grandé, available in hardtop format only, was standard with the 200-ci six-cylinder engine like the base hardtop. The price started at $2,849.

Exterior Styling and Features

The new Mustang's bodywork was completely new, so Ford went to work educating the consumers on the virtues of its new pony car:

- Dual 5-inch horizontal headlights and a matte black, injection-molded plastic, and egg-crate grille were highlighted by the distinctive tri-color Mustang emblem mounted in a off-center position.
- A wider C-pillar and tunneled backlight combined to create more of a formal roofline (hardtop models).
- Ventless front side windows improved appearance and increased driver/passenger visibility.
- Simulated air exhausts with a bright metal horizontal bar grille were incorporated into the quarter panels.
- Parking lights were recessed into an air slot in the front splash panel below a streamlined front bumper.

- SportsRoof models featured a sleek new roofline complemented by a built-in rear deck spoiler and deep simulated side air scoops.
- Convertible models featured a change in the folding top mechanism that provided a larger rear quarter window and allowed the top to stack nearly flush with the beltline.
- Grandé models featured "Grandé" script lettering on the C-pillar, dual color-keyed racing mirrors, wire wheel covers, bright wheel lip, rocker panel, rear deck moldings, and a special two-toned narrow paint stripe below the fender line.

What's more "in your face" than a Calypso Coral Boss 302? Not much! This one is all stock, aside from the owner-added replica Torq-Thrust wheels.

The back window glass on all hardtops was encircled with a black surround, regardless of body color.

A 1969 Boss 429 in Wimbledon White takes a breather in the rural Colorado countryside.

The Boss 302 grille was standard Mustang issue with the tri-shield/pony emblem off-center for 1969.

- Mach 1 featured a special two-toned hood with a simulated air scoop, exposed hood lock pins, dual color-keyed racing mirrors, tape stripes on the spoiler and body side, E70x14 white sidewall tires, pop-open gas cap (without the GT emblem), chrome styled steel wheels, and dual exhaust with bright extensions when equipped with the 351 4V or larger engine.

- Boss 302 external highlights included: low-gloss black paint on hood and cowl area; a blacked-out headlight-housing area; front spoiler; special "Boss 302" reflective C-stripes on body side; low-gloss black paint on the deck lid and rear panel between the taillights; flared front fenders that were rolled under to provide more room for F60x15 tires; 15-inch Magnum 500 wheels;

1969 STANDARD EQUIPMENT

- Accelerator pedal: suspended type
- Alternator: 38 amps
- Armrests: front
- Ashtray: front
- Backup lights
- Battery: Autolite Sta-Ful design, 45 amps
- Body: rust resistant and insulated
- Bucket seats: foam padded, adjustable
- Carpets: 100 percent nylon, molded
- Choke: automatic
- Cigarette lighter
- Coolant: two years or 36,000 miles
- Courtesy lights: door switches
- Door checks: two stages
- Door hinges: bronze, bushed
- Door trim: all vinyl
- Emergency flashers
- Engine: 200 Six
- Exhaust emission control system (all engines)
- Finish: Super Diamond Lustre Enamel
- Front fenders: bolt-on
- Fuel tank: 20 gallons
- Glass: safety laminated windshield
- Glass: safety, solid tempered, side and rear
- Glove box: instrument panel mounted
- Head restraints: adjustable front seats
- Headlights: dual
- Headlining: color-keyed vinyl
- Heater and defroster: fresh air
- Hood latch: single action
- Jack: scissors type
- Lamps, bulbs: extended life
- Lubrication, chassis: 36,000 miles or 36 months
- Mirror: outside rearview
- Muffler: aluminized and stainless steel
- Scuff plates: aluminum
- Thermostat: 195 degrees Fahrenheit
- Transmission: three-speed manual
- Transmission lever: tunnel mounted
- Upholstery: all vinyl
- Valve lifters: hydraulic (except Boss 302)
- Ventilation: cowl side
- Vent-less side glass
- Windshield washers
- Windshield wipers: two-speed electric

and a filled-in quarter panel simulated air scoop. Boss 302s were available in SportsRoof body style only.

- Boss 429 exterior styling cues included the largest hood scoop ever installed on a Mustang (color-keyed to match the body); a unique front spoiler; flared front fenders that were rolled under to provide more room for F60x15 tires; special "Boss 429" decals mounted on the front fenders; 15-inch Magnum 500 wheels; and dual color-keyed racing mirrors.

The GT Equipment Group ($146.71) was available for one last time as a 1969 model equipment option. It was available for all body styles, but it could only be ordered with a 351-ci or larger

The standard twist-off gas cap for 1969 was simple in design. It remained in its traditional position in the center of the rear panel.

Sport slats were first available only on 1969 Boss 302s. In 1970, they were offered on all SportsRoof model Mustangs.

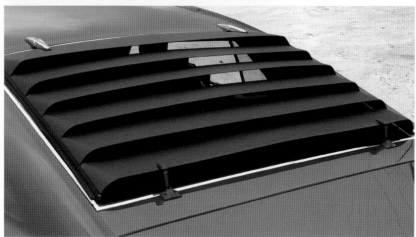

Rear and front side markers were lights in 1969, as opposed to the reflectors on 1968 models.

The hood scoop was nonfunctional on 351-equipped Mach 1s.

BODY SPECIFICATIONS

	Hardtop	Fastback	Convertible
Length (overall, inches)	187.4	187.46	187.4
Width (overall, inches)	71.3	71.3	71.3
Height (overall, inches)	51.2	51.2	51.2
Wheelbase (overall)	108	108	108
Curb weight (pounds)	2,835	2,860	2,945

(six cylinder, standard transmission)

VIN/TRIM/DSO TAG DECODING FOR 1969

Model Year Code
9=1969

Assembly Plant Codes
F= Dearborn, Michigan
R= San Jose, California
T= Metuchen, New Jersey

Body Serial Codes
01= hardtop   02= fastback   03= convertible

Engine Codes
F= 302-ci eight-cylinder, 2 bbl
G= 302-ci eight-cylinder, 4 bbl (Boss 302)
H= 351-ci eight-cylinder, 2 bbl
L= 250-ci six-cylinder, 1 bbl
M= 351-ci eight-cylinder, 4 bbl
Q= 428-ci eight-cylinder, 4 bbl
R= 428-ci eight-cylinder, 4 bbl (Ram Air)
S= 390-ci eight-cylinder, 4 bbl
T= 200-ci six-cylinder, 1 bbl
Z= 429-ci eight-cylinder, 4 bbl (Boss 429)

Consecutive Number
The remaining six digits in the VIN indicate the vehicle's consecutive unit number assigned at the production line.

BODY STYLE CODES

63A= fastback standard (bucket seat)
63B= fastback Decor Group (bucket seat)
63C= fastback standard (Mach 1)
65A= hardtop standard (bucket seat)
65B= hardtop Decor Group (bucket seat)
65C= hardtop standard (bench seat)
65D= hardtop Decor Group (bench seat)
65E= hardtop Grandé
76A= convertible standard (bucket seat)
76B= convertible Decor Group (bucket seat)

COLOR CODES

2= New Lime
6= Pastel Gray
B= Royal Maroon
D= Acapulco Blue
F= Gulfstream Aqua
M= Wimbledon White
S= Champagne Gold
W= Meadowlark Yellow
4= Silver Jade
A= Raven Black
C= Black Jade
E= Aztec Aqua
I= Lime Gold
P= Winter Blue
T= Candyapple Red
Y= Indian Fire

TRIM CODES

Hardtop, SportsRoof, Convertible (Bucket Seats)
2A= Black 2B= Blue 2D= Red 2G= Ivy Gold 2Y= Nugget Gold

Hardtop, SportsRoof, Convertible (Hi-Back Bucket Seats, Comfortweave)
4A= Black 4D= Red

Hardtop, SportsRoof, Convertible (Hi-Back Bucket Seats, Comfortweave, Decor Group)
DA= Black DD= Red DW= White

Hardtop, SportsRoof (Comfortweave Vinyl Deluxe Bucket Seats)
5A= Black 5B= Blue 5D= Red 5G= Ivy Gold 5W= White 5Y= Nugget Gold

Hardtop (Comfortweave Vinyl Bench Seat)
8A= Black 8B= Blue 8D= Red 8Y= Nugget Gold

Hardtop (Comfortweave Vinyl Bench Seat, Decor Group)
9A= Black 9B= Blue 9D= Red 9Y= Nugget Gold

Convertible (Deluxe All-Vinyl Bucket Seats)
7A= Black 7B= Blue 7D= Red 7G= Ivy Gold 7W= White 7Y= Nugget Gold

Grandé Hardtop (Luxury Cloth and Vinyl)
1A= Black 1B= Blue 1G= Ivy Gold 1Y= Nugget Gold

Mach 1 SportsRoof (Comfortweave Vinyl Bucket Seats)
Black= 3A Red= 3D White= 3W

DATE CODES

The number (1–31) appearing before the month letter indicates the day.

Month	First Year	Second Year
January	A	N
February	B	P
March	C	Q
April	D	R
May	E	S
June	F	T
July	G	U
August	H	V
September	J	W
October	K	X
November	L	Y
December	M	Z

DSO CODES

This code indicates the city/area in which the vehicle was originally destined for delivery.

11= Boston, Massachusetts
13= New York City, New York
15= Newark, New Jersey
16= Philadelphia, Pennsylvania
17= Washington, D.C.
21= Atlanta, Georgia
22= Charlotte, North Carolina
24= Jacksonville, Florida
25= Richmond, Virginia
28= Louisville, Kentucky
32= Cleveland, Ohio
33= Detroit, Michigan
35= Lansing, Michigan
37= Buffalo, New York
38= Pittsburgh, Pennsylvania
41= Chicago, Illinois
43= Milwaukee, Wisconsin
44= Twin Cities, Minneapolis
46= Indianapolis
47= Cincinnati, Ohio
51= Denver, Colorado
53= Kansas City, Missouri
54= Omaha, Nebraska
55= St. Louis, Missouri
56= Davenport, Iowa
61= Dallas, Texas
62= Houston, Texas
63= Memphis, Tennessee
64= New Orleans, Louisiana
65= Oklahoma City, Oklahoma
71= Los Angeles, California
72= San Jose, California
73= Salt Lake City, Utah
74= Seattle, Washington
75= Phoenix, Arizona
83= Government
84= Home Office Reserve
85= American Red Cross
89= Transportation Services
90–99= Export

FAR LEFT: The pop-open gas cap was standard on the Mach 1.

LEFT: This rare find is the pop-open gas cap from a 1969 Mustang GT. The GT production was way down in 1969 with the advent of the Mach 1 and Boss cars. The year 1969 was the last year for the GT.

Dual color-keyed racing mirrors were standard on the Mach 1.

Boss 302s came without any form of side scoop in 1969. All other Mustang models, including the Boss 429, featured side scoops.

AXLE CODES

Conventional	Limited Slip	Axle Ratio
1	J	2.50
2	K	2.75
3	L	2.79
4	M	2.80
5	N	2.83
6	O	3.00
7	P	3.10
8	Q	3.20
9	R	3.25
A	S	3.50
B	T	3.07
C	U	3.08
D	V	3.91
E	W	4.30

TRANSMISSION CODES

1= three-speed manual
5= four-speed manual wide-ratio (2.78 first gear)
6= four-speed manual close-ratio (2.32 first gear)
U= automatic (C6)   W= automatic (C4)
X= automatic (FMX)   Y= automatic (MX)

engine. The package included a GT racing stripe that was applied to the rocker panel area, but it did not include a GT or Mustang emblem. The stripe was only available in four colors: Black, White, Red, or Gold. The GT package also included a pop-open fuel filler cap, a nonfunctional hood scoop (a functional Shaker scoop was included when ordered with the 428 Cobra Jet with Ram Air engine), pin-type hood latches, styled steel wheels with E70x14 white sidewall tires, GT emblems in wheel center caps, dual exhaust (included with four-barrel engines only), and heavy-duty suspension (including a heavier front sway bar).

The Exterior Decor Group ($32.44) was back as an option for 1969 and available for the hardtop, SportsRoof, and convertible models. It included wheel lip opening moldings, rocker panel moldings, rear end moldings, and base five-spoke wheel covers.

Large, reflective side tape stripes left no doubt as to what kind of Mustang they belonged on!

The Boss 302's chin spoiler was different than that of the Mach 1 and Boss 429, no doubt due to its role in Trans Am–style racing.

SportsRoof style Mustangs, other than Boss 302, all featured aggressive-looking simulated side air scoops.

Turn-signal indicators were integral in the back of the hood scoops for 1969.

Interior

With the advent of a total restyling exercise for the 1969 model year came a completely restyled interior. This was no simple refresh job; the new Mustang's insides were gone through from scratch. No longer did you feel like you were sitting in a mid-1960s car. Everything was bigger, thicker, and more cavelike for 1969. The car was longer and wider, and when nestled inside the completely new pony car, one certainly was reminded of that fact!

Ford's "Interior Features" section in its sales literature talked about the changes: "Mustang interiors have been completely redesigned for added driver and passenger comfort and convenience."

The new features of interior included:

- New door and quarter section design for more shoulder, hip, and leg room
- Double hood instrument panel forms and individual type panel area for both driver and passenger
- Four-pod design instrument cluster groups, with all instruments and controls within easy reach and view of the driver
- Energy absorbing armrests housing the squeeze-type door handles that were recessed for added protection
- Standard bucket seats made of thick-padded molded urethane covered in durable vinyl that came in Black, Blue, Red, Ivy Gold, Nugget Gold, or White (Deluxe Interior Group only)
- Grandé's interior included: hopsack cloth and vinyl seat trim; simulated teakwood grained instrument panel and cluster appliqué; deluxe three-spoke, rim-blow steering wheel (included simulated teakwood trim and rim-blow horn); molded door panels with courtesy lights; padded interior quarter trim panels with armrests; electric clock with sweep second hand; and bright-trimmed pedal pads
- Mach 1's interior featured: all-new high-back bucket seats with Comfortweave knitted vinyl inserts; a deluxe three-spoke, rim-blow steering wheel; special carpeting with a red accent stripe on black interior trim; a floor console with simulated teakwood grain trim; instrument panel and door panels; molded door trim panels with courtesy lamps; an electric clock; and bright-trimmed pedal pads

The all-new-for-1969 instrument panel really did give you the feel of being in a cockpit. You sat low in the seat and were directly facing four large pods that were set deep in the instrument panel and in a black camera case plastic housing.

ABOVE: The base interior for 1969. The owner added a woodgrain steering wheel rim.

RIGHT: Base door panels for 1969. The door handle was now located in the armrest.

BELOW RIGHT: This is the standard AM radio installed in 1969 Mach 1.

The two inner pods were larger in diameter than the two outer pods, and a four-pod instrument panel contained the alternator gauge, speedometer, fuel/coolant, and oil pressure. Arrow-shaped turn indicator lights were located in the outer smaller pods.

The Interior Decor Group (priced at $101.10 and not available on Grandé and Mach 1) included deluxe seat trim with Comfortweave knitted vinyl inserts, carpeted lower door panels, courtesy door lights, deluxe three-spoke steering wheel with rim-blow horn, and a chrome-finished driver's side remote rearview mirror.

The Deluxe Interior Decor Group ($133.44, convertible and SportsRoof only) featured items in the Interior Decor Group along with simulated woodgrain instrument panel appliqués, dark gray gauge faces, and the numbers on the speedometer in increments of five.

ABOVE: The interior of the Mach 1 was very upscale and featured many of the items found in the Interior Decor Group. Note the color-keyed floor inserts.

RIGHT: The rear seat area in Mach 1 or any SportsRoof model was for storage or kids only. The owner added rear sports slats. FAR RIGHT: High-back bucket seats with Comfortweave option in a Boss 302.

RIGHT: High-back bucket seats with Comfortweave option in a Mach 1. Note the color accent trim.
FAR RIGHT: The full-length doorjamb sill plates were a different design than the previous year.

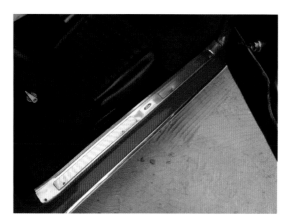

The 351-ci, four-barrel V-8 as it sits in a 1969 Mach 1. The base engine for Mach 1 was the 351 two-barrel.

Neither of these packages was available for the Grandé or Mach 1, since both models included decor items as standard equipment.

All Mustang interior options were available for the Boss 302 for 1969. Boss 429s came standard with the Interior Decor Group.

Other popular interior options included an 8,000-rpm tachometer, which featured a gray-faced tachometer for the Deluxe Interior Decor Group, while the standard interior tach face was black with white numbers. The radio options were AM, AM/FM, and AM/eight-track tape. Other options included high-back bucket seats, bench seat, console, electric clock, visibility group, SelectAire air conditioning, power ventilation, intermittent windshield wipers, deluxe seat and shoulder belts, tilt-away steering wheel, rear seat speaker (hardtop only), and speed control. For a complete listing of all options, see the options chart in this chapter.

Chassis

As described in Chapter 1, "the platform carries the body on the top, encloses the engine, and provides attaching points for the various chassis components. It also provides the basic structure of the car. The platform is made up of a box-section front and rear side rails tied in securely to heavy boxed-in rocker panels. These components are connected by five heavy gauge crossmembers to form an extra strong ladder-type framing under the car. The front and rear side rails extend partially under, and are welded to, the floor pan. The full-depth, full-length tunnel down the center of the floor pan adds a backbone to give the structure maximum rigidity. The full-depth side panels in the engine compartment are welded to the front side rails at the bottom and to the cowl at the rear. The tops of these panels were pressed over to form a wide flange and increase front end rigidity. A one-piece stamping with a deep channel section at the top connects the inside panels across the front."

Regardless of the car's engine size, all Mustangs were based on the same platform chassis. Upgraded suspension components compensated for the weight differences in engines.

Engines

200-ci Six
The 200-ci six-cylinder engine was unchanged as standard equipment on all Mustang models for 1969.

The 428 Cobra Jet. This particular engine happens to be a Super Cobra Jet with beefed-up components. All these components were provided when either the V-code (3.91:1) or W-code (4.30:1) axle ratios were ordered.

Quick facts:

- Seven main bearings: smoother engine operation, less vibration, longer engine life
- Hydraulic valve lifters: quiet operation, low maintenance
- Large valves: more efficient breathing, more seat area for better cooling and less burning
- Short stroke design: less vibration, less wear.
- Single-venturi carburetor: economical operation
- Six-month or 6,000-mile oil filter: reduced maintenance, improved oil filtering
- Automatic choke: sensed ambient and coolant temperatures; helped prevent flooding on semiwarm starts
- 8.8:1 compression ratio: better efficiency on regular or economy gasoline
- Thin wall casting: better cooling, less weight

- Precision-molded crankshaft: dependable, smooth operation
- Weather-insulated ignition system: reliable starts under all climatic conditions

250-ci Six

The big news for Mustang for 1969 was the introduction of the 250 engine, also known as the Big Six. Ford was pretty excited about this new offering for 1969 and told the world in its sales literature: "Ford's 1969 engine story is headlined by the all-new 4.1-liter, 250-ci engine . . . another 'Better Idea' innovation. Designed with emission control features as part of its basic concept, this new engine is exceptionally lightweight and efficient with a 'nearly square' bore to stroke dimension of 3.68 inches to 3.91 inches. New engine mounts on the 250 engine furnish much

BASE EQUIPMENT ENGINE: T-CODE

- Bore and stroke: 3.68x3.13
- Carburetor: Autolite 1100, 1V
- Compression ratio: 8.8:1
- Displacement: 200 ci
- Horsepower: 115 at 3,800 rpm
- Torque: 190 ft-lbs at 2,200 rpm
- Type: inline six-cylinder, overhead valve
- Valve lifters: hydraulic

OPTIONAL EQUIPMENT ENGINE: L-CODE

- Bore and stroke: 3.68x3.91
- Carburetor: Autolite 1100, 1V
- Compression ratio: 9.0:1
- Displacement: 250 ci
- Horsepower: 155 at 4,400 rpm
- Torque: 240 ft-lbs at 1,600 rpm
- Type: inline six-cylinder, overhead valve
- Valve lifters: hydraulic

smoother operation from idle to full-throttle. The 250 is standard in the Fairlane and optional in the Mustang."

Quick facts:

- Designed for emission control: the design resulted in a more effective combustion process than added-on emission control equipment in comparable engines in the 250-ci range.
- Nearly square bore-to-stroke dimensions: the 3.68 to 3.91 ratio had a compact combustion chamber configuration that efficiently utilized the fuel and reduces exhaust emission.
- Closed crankcase ventilation: designed for efficient reburning of combustion gases; system had a closed, recirculating circuit that prevented escape of fumes or combustion gases from the engine crankcase.
- Hot and cold air cleaner system: the system sensed its own intake air temperature needs and selected either manifold-heated air or outside air; resulted in efficient fuel combustion and economy, improved performance, and virtual elimination of stalls due to carburetor icing; more precise calibration of the carburetor because of the narrow range of incoming air temperature.
- Controlled automatic choke: choke operation was automatically controlled by both engine temperature and vacuum conditions to utilize exhaust heat and improve starting and cold drive-away performance
- Larger water pump bearings: the bearing size was increased to ¾-inch diameter for improved durability and operation.

302-ci V-8 2V

The 302-ci two-barrel V-8 that was introduced in 1968 continued on into 1969 Mustangs. The J-code 302 four-barrel version was no longer available.

Quick facts:

- Molded crankshaft: extra engine stability, smoother operating
- Connecting rods and pistons: short connecting rods with extrastrength design, deep skirt pistons with tolerance for longer engine wear

OPTIONAL EQUIPMENT ENGINE: F-CODE

- Bore and stroke: 4.00x3.00
- Carburetor: Ford 2100 (280 cfm), 2V
- Compression ratio: 9.5:1
- Displacement: 302 ci
- Horsepower: 220 at 4,600 rpm
- Torque: 300 ft-lbs at 2,600 rpm
- Type: eight cylinder, overhead valve
- Valve lifters: hydraulic

- Hot and cold dual inlet cleaner system: reduced throttle plate icing in cold weather, improved engine operation required for emission control
- Full-length, full-circle water jackets: uniform cylinder temperature with a minimum of hot spots
- High-capacity fuel filter: inline design to provide maximum filtration
- Hydraulic valve lifters: no adjustment required
- Dual advance distributor: correct spark advance for all driving conditions
- Six-month or 6,000-mile oil filter: reduced maintenance, improved oil filtering
- Lightweight cast-iron construction: advanced thin wall castings

351-ci V-8 2V and 4V (Windsor based)

The 351 made its debut in the 1969 Mustangs as two- and four-barrel versions. Ford Motor Company advertised these engines as: "Precision-cast for strength in the manner developed for lightweight racing engines, the 351-ci V-8 engine offers a weight advantage over competitive engines in the same displacement range. A completely new cylinder block has been incorporated into the 351, as well as the features developed and proved in the other Ford V-8 engines. The 2V and 4V versions are optional equipment on Fairlane and Mustang."

Quick facts (highlights):

- New design cylinder block: The precision-cast, advanced thin wall racing engine design was compact with a reduced weight-to-displacement ratio for better economy and performance.
- Hot and cold air cleaner design: Thermostat-controlled valve selected manifold heated air or air from the engine

OPTIONAL EQUIPMENT ENGINE: H-CODE

- Bore and stroke: 4.00x3.50
- Carburetor: Ford 2100 (350 cfm), 2V
- Compression ratio: 9.5:1
- Displacement: 351 ci
- Horsepower: 250 at 4,600 rpm
- Torque: 355 ft-lbs at 2,600 rpm
- Type: eight cylinder, overhead valve
- Valve lifters: hydraulic

OPTIONAL EQUIPMENT ENGINE: M-CODE

- Bore and stroke: 4.00x3.50
- Carburetor: Ford 4300 (470 cfm), 4V
- Compression ratio: 10.7:1
- Displacement: 351 ci
- Horsepower: 290 at 4,800 rpm
- Torque: 385 ft-lbs at 3,200 rpm
- Type: eight cylinder, overhead valve
- Valve lifters: hydraulic

The Boss 302 4V for 1969. This high-winding, small block pumped out 290 horses and 290 ft-lbs of torque.

compartment to provide better vaporization of the fuel and reduces icing.

- Sand cast intake manifold: Cast of iron alloy manifold had equal length intake passages; exhaust flow through the manifold between cylinder banks preheated the incoming fuel-air mixture for more complete vaporization.
- Full-length water jackets: Provided uniform cylinder temperatures; allowed a higher, more economical overall engine operating temperature; and reduced preignition caused by hot spots.
- Precision shell-molded crankshaft: Made of nodular iron and precision cast for high strength and minimum weight, it provided ideal placement of counterweights for smoother operation; six integral counter-weights plus an external counterweight were at each end in the five-main-bearing design.
- Lightweight pistons: Precision-machined, aluminum alloy pistons had a slipper skirt design and imbedded steel struts to provide less weight, longer life, and controlled expansion of the piston during high-speed operation.
- High-lift camshaft: Precision-molded of special nodular alloy iron with a chain drive and five replaceable insert bearings

maximized performance without sacrificing fuel economy.

- Preset hydraulic valve lifters: No adjustment was required; utilized high-pressure oil from the engine lubrication system to keep each lifter continuously in contact with its cam and valve lifter body; chrome-plated tappet plungers gave greater resistance to wear and corrosion.

390-ci V-8 4V

With the advent of the 351 and 428 engines, 1969 was the last year for the venerable 390 powerplant in the Mustang line.

Quick facts:

- Chrome dress-up kit: standard on the 325 horsepower version; included chrome-plated air cleaner, valve covers, oil filter, dip stick, and radiator cap
- Full-flow fuel filter: inline design to provide maximum filtration
- High-performance valve springs and damper assembly: greater resistance to fatigue and wear
- Six-month or 6,000-mile oil filter: reduced maintenance, improved oil filtering
- Compression ratio of 10.5:1: maximum power from premium fuels

OPTIONAL EQUIPMENT ENGINE: S-CODE (GT)

- Bore and stroke: 4.05x3.78
- Carburetor: Ford 4300 (600 cfm), 4V
- Compression ratio: 10.5:1
- Displacement: 390 ci
- Horsepower: 320 at 4,400 rpm
- Torque: 427 ft-lbs at 3,200 rpm
- Type: eight cylinder, overhead valve
- Valve lifters: hydraulic

- Camshaft lobe profile: more usable torque with a smooth idle
- Dual advance distributor: corrected spark advance for all driving conditions
- Lightweight, cast-iron construction: used advanced thin wall casting techniques
- Alternate valve spacing: higher volumetric efficiency, elimination of hot spots in cylinder block and heads
- Free-flow exhaust system: large exhaust passages, individual exhaust header to minimize exhaust pressure, twin pipes and mufflers
- Short stroke design: less friction, longer engine life
- Low-capacity oil sump: four-quart design gave better circulation and cooling

428-ci V-8 4V (Ram Air and non-Ram Air)

The 428 Cobra Jet engine that was introduced in the 1968 Mustang continued on into 1969 both as Ram Air and non–Ram Air versions. Non–Ram Air versions were designated Q-codes and fitted with a standard snorkel-type air cleaner. The Ram Air version was equipped with an air cleaner assembly with a vacuum-actuated bypass inlet valve mounted in the top.

OPTIONAL EQUIPMENT ENGINE: Q-CODE (NON-RAM AIR)

- Bore and stroke: 4.13x3.98
- Carburetor: Holley 4150 (735 cfm), 4V
- Compression ratio: 10.6:1
- Displacement: 428 ci
- Horsepower: 335 at 5,200 rpm
- Torque: 445 ft-lbs at 3,400 rpm
- Type: eight cylinder, overhead valve
- Valve lifters: hydraulic

OPTIONAL EQUIPMENT ENGINE: R-CODE (RAM AIR)

- Bore and stroke: 4.13x3.98
- Carburetor: Holley 4150 (735 cfm), 4V
- Compression ratio: 10.6:1
- Displacement: 428 ci
- Horsepower: 335 at 5,200 rpm
- Torque: 445 ft-lbs at 3,400 rpm
- Type: eight cylinder, overhead valve
- Valve lifters: hydraulic

Quick facts:
- Full-length, full-circle water jackets: designed to take advantage of thin wall casting and permitted higher overall engine operating temperature for increased performance capabilities
- New exhaust header-type manifolds: larger inside dimensions and extended runner lengths blended into a larger collection chamber to help extract exhaust gases, especially in the high-rpm capabilities of the 428s
- Electronically balanced crankshaft: a vibration damper, floated and mounted on rubber, on the front end of the crankshaft counteracted torsional vibration and provided smoother operation
- Heavy-duty valve springs: allowed the engine to exceed 5,000 rpm without encountering valve float
- Special high lift camshaft: stepped bearings reduced any possibility of damage during assembly; cam lobes were precision ground to provide maximum power at high rpm
- Dual advance distributor: correct spark advance was maintained for all driving conditions; centrifugal advance plus vacuum-controlled advance permitted more precise distributor calibration for a more efficient engine operation
- Full-flow fuel filter: maximum filtration was provided with minimum restriction for higher efficiency and power output

Starting with the 1969 model year, a version of the 428 Cobra Jet was known as the Super Cobra Jet (SCJ) engine. It was an upgraded unit when the V-code (3.91:1) or W-code (4.30:1) axle ratios were ordered. The SCJs were manufactured with a more durable reciprocating assembly (crank, rods, pistons, flywheel, flexplate, harmonic balancer). SCJ engines received 427 LeMans cap-screw connecting rods, and an external oil cooler was mounted in front of the radiator. Officially speaking, the SCJ horsepower ratings were the same as the basic CJ versions. Starting in mid-1969, this option was known as the Drag Pack.

302-ci V-8 4V (Boss 302)

What can be said about the legendary Boss 302? Plenty! Ford developed this hot little powerplant primarily for open-track competition in the Trans Am road racing circuit. Here is what FoMoCo had to say about it: "The 302-ci 4V V-8 is a true international formula engine falling in the important 5-liter class. In the United States and Canada, the Trans-Am 5-liter sedan races are among the most numerous in the big time circuit

OPTIONAL EQUIPMENT ENGINE: G-CODE (BOSS 302)

- Bore and stroke: 4.00x3.00
- Compression ratio: 10.6:1
- Carburetor: Holley 4150 (780 cfm) 4V
- Displacement: 302 ci
- Horsepower: 290 at 5,800 rpm
- Torque: 290 ft-lbs at 4,300 rpm
- Type: eight cylinder, overhead valve
- Valve lifters: solid

and the importance of this size powerplant continues to grow. The 302 Boss is rated at 290 horsepower at 5,800 rpm and is available only in the Boss 302 Mustang SportsRoof model."

Quick facts:

- Cylinder heads: broader to accommodate the canted valves and splayed rocker arms; canted valves improved gas flow, allowed larger-diameter valves, and provided room between the pushrods, large $\frac{7}{16}$-inch UBS

The four-speed transmission (Toploader) was connected to a massive 428 SCJ engine. The owner added the woodgrain steering wheel rim.

The four-speed shifter in the upscale Mach 1.

head bolts were used to fasten the heads to the block for an extra margin of strength

- Forged crankshaft: specially balanced at higher than normal speeds to accommodate the capacity of this powerplant; four-bolt main bearing caps strengthened the foundation of the engine
- Connecting rods: heavy-duty with $\frac{3}{8}$-inch nut and bolt fasteners
- Intake manifold: aluminum free-flow designed with large runners to match the cylinder heads
- Valve covers: chrome-plated

429-ci V-8 4V (Boss 429)

The Boss 429 engine (385 series) was a 429 Cobra Jet engine with some serious revisions intended for NASCAR competition on the super speedways. Ford described it in a special supplemental brochure: "The 429 Boss is the all-out race version (of the 429 engine series) which, in modified form, has successfully campaigned the stock car circuit in the NASCAR-winning Torinos."

The engine had an aluminum head and transverse valve placement that resulted in a crescent-shaped combustion chamber. The splayed rocker arms accommodated the outboard and inboard valve positions in order to make room for the large intake ports. Other features of the engine were a high-rise aluminum intake manifold with large runners matching the head ports, a 735-cfm 4V Holley carburetor, header exhaust manifolds, and cast-aluminum valve covers. Lightweight alloys helped keep down the weight of the engine.

OPTIONAL EQUIPMENT ENGINE: Z-CODE (BOSS 429)

- Bore and stroke: 4.36x3.59
- Carburetor: Holley 4150 (735 cfm), 4V
- Compression ratio: 10.5:1
- Displacement: 429 ci
- Horsepower: 375 at 5,200 rpm
- Torque: 450 ft-lbs at 3,400 rpm
- Type: eight cylinder, overhead valve • Valve lifters: hydraulic (on "S" and early "T" versions)

Transmissions

For 1969, the base transmission was the three-speed manual. This fully synchronized transmission was standard on all Mustang models except Boss 302 and Boss 429, which were both equipped with the close-ratio, quick-shifting, four-speed transmissions.

A four-speed manual transmission was optional with all engines except the 200-ci six-cylinder. The transmission was fully synchronized in all forward gears and permitted upshifts and downshifts at speed without gear clash or noise.

The SelectShift Cruise-O-Matic transmission was a fully automatic unit, available as optional equipment in all Mustang models except the Boss 302 and Boss 429. This transmission also permitted manual shifting.

Suspension, Steering, and Brakes

Front Suspension

The merits of the suspension on the 1969 Mustangs were described by Ford as: "Mustang uses a short and long arm ball joint front suspension. Springs and shocks are calibrated to match the weight/ride requirements of each application, depending on the car model, engine, and optional equipment."

The front suspension features included:

- Single lower drag strut stabilizer arm was mounted to the frame through rubber bushings to eliminate metal-to-metal contact and reduce the amount of vibration and noise transmitted to the passenger area.
- This drag strut was anchored in a rubber bushing that allowed the wheels to move slightly toward the rear when hitting a bump. The controlled rear movement absorbed part of the initial road shock before it reached the passenger area.
- A link-type, rubber-bushed stabilizer bar connected the right- and left-hand lower suspension arms and prevented excessive lean when cornering.

Rear Suspension

Mustang's Hotchkiss-type rear suspension featured rubber bushings at connection points to prevent metal-to-metal contact and minimize noise transfer to the passenger compartment. Features of the system included:

- Long 53-inch, multileaf springs smoothed out driving and braking forces to provide a comfortable, cushioned ride.
- Front spring mounting eye incorporated a large resilient rubber bushing that allowed slight horizontal wheel movement to help absorb small bumps and reduce road shock and noise.
- Rear spring shackle was a rubber-bushed compression type that flexed on light impact and provided greater resistance to severe impact.
- Shock absorbers were mounted at an angle to reduce side sway and improve control. A constant viscosity fluid was used to provide uniform performance under all climatic conditions.
- The competition suspension had a staggered shock arrangement designed to control spring windup and wheel hop. The left shock absorber was relocated to the rear of the axle, and the right shock remained ahead of the axle.

Steering

The Mustang's manual steering system in 1969 models was a parallelogram linkage type with a cross link and idler arm. The system offered more control under all driving conditions with a minimum of steering effort.

Features of the steering system included:

- Cross link bar positioned to improve directional stability and reduce oversteer.
- Steering shaft control assembly was driven by recirculating ball bearings in a closed channel for reduced friction. The Magic-Circle steering gear was filled with a lifetime lubricant that didn't need to be changed under normal circumstances.

Power Steering

Power steering was optional for all 1969 Mustang models. The system utilized the standard manual steering linkage. The cross link had a ball joint stud attachment that was integrated with the power cylinder assembly.

Features of the unit included a built-in low-restriction feature of the control valve that allowed the front wheels to return to the center position after making a turn. A 20.5:1 overall steering ratio provided responsive steering and reduced steering effort.

Brakes

All Mustangs for 1969 were equipped with a dual hydraulic brake system. The standard brakes on all cars were a duo-servo design—self-energizing, single anchor, internal expanding, and air cooled. The linings were self-adjusting when the brakes were applied while the car was moving in reverse. Front wheel power disc brakes were optional on all V-8-powered Mustangs.

Heating and Ventilation

For 1969, the venting system was radically changed on the Mustang. The new system provided improved ventilation for comfort when the windows were up, and it operated just as well on the move or at a standstill. Using the air inlet and blower provided with the heater, a special duct was added to direct cool air through a high-level center register. A vacuum-operated valve in the duct opened when the control lever was switched to "power vent." The air stream could be directed across the interior by setting the blower speed and adjusting the register vents. The

For 1969, the heater controls were located centrally and under the radio. Air conditioning controls were located in the same integral unit. This particular car is not equipped with air conditioning.

The radiator handled the cooling with the help of a 195-degree Fahrenheit thermostat.

control for forced ventilation was integrated to permit either cool outside air or heated air to be directed out of the vents. The controls for the unit were located near the bottom of the instrument panel.

The SelectAire air conditioner was an option for 1969 and had an MSRP of $379.57. As stated on the RPO list, SelectAire was not available for Mustangs equipped with the 200-ci six or the 428-ci with four-speed manual transmissions.

Wheels and Tires

The standard 1969 Mustang wheel was a 14x5-inch stamped steel unit with vent holes. Mustangs equipped with a six-cylinder engine had wheels with a four-lug bolt pattern. The standard tire was C78x14. Mustangs equipped with 390-ci and 428-ci V-8s came with 14x6 wheels and 7.35x14 tires. The base wheel cover was a simulated spoke-type full cover. Boss 302 and Boss 429 Mustangs came with F60x15 superwide oval tires that were mounted on chrome-plated Magnum 500 wheels.

Optional wheels included wire wheel cover, argent styled steel, chrome styled steel wheel, and color-keyed styled steel wheel. The wire wheel cover was standard on the Grandé and available as an option on all other models except Mach 1, Boss 302, and Boss 429.

The argent styled steel was a racing-style steel wheel that had an argent finish, bright hubcap, and chrome trim ring. It was included in the GT Equipment Group and optional on all other models. When it was ordered on a GT-equipped Mustang, a GT identification was included in the hubcap.

The chrome-plated styled steel wheel and hubcap was standard on the Mach 1 and optional on all other models except Grandé. When it was ordered on GT Equipment Group models, the "GT" lettering appeared in the center hub.

The color-keyed styled steel wheel was color-matched to the Mustang's body color and was available as an option on all models except Grandé. Bright polished trim rings surrounded the ventilation slots. The hub area was chrome, and when ordered on GT Equipment Group models, the "GT" lettering appeared in the center hub.

Shelby Mustangs

Body

The all-new-for-1969 Mustang resulted in an all-new Shelby. The car was starting to look less and less like a Mustang. Instead of the pointed front end that the 1967 and 1968 Shelbys possessed, the 1969 model's nose looked square and chopped off. An all-new fiberglass hood was fitted with

REGULAR PRODUCTION OPTIONS

250-ci 155-horsepower Six (not available with Mach I)	25.91
302-ci 220-horsepower V-8 (not available with Mach I)	105.00
Extra Charge Over 302-ci V-8 for:	
351-ci 250-horsepower V-8 (standard on Mach I)	58.34
351-ci 290-horsepower 4V V-8 (except Mach I)	84.25
390-ci 320-horsepower V-8 (except Mach I)	158.08
428-ci over 335-horsepower V-8 (except Mach I)	287.53
428-ci 335-horsepower Ram Air Cobra Jet V-8 (except Mach I)	420.96
Adjustable head restraints (not available with Mach I)	17.00
AM/FM stereo radio	181.36
Chrome styled steel wheels (standard on Mach I; not available with Grandé or 200-ci engine)	116.59
Chrome styled steel wheels with Exterior Decor Group	95.31
Chrome styled steel wheels with GT Group	77.73
Color-keyed dual racing mirrors	19.48
Competition suspension (available with 428 only; standard with Mach I and GT)	30.64
Console	53.82
Convertible glass rear window	38.86
Deluxe belts with reminder light	15.59
Deluxe Interior Decor Group (SportsRoof and convertible)	133.44
Deluxe Interior Decor Group with dual racing mirror option	120.48
Electric clock (standard on Mach I and Grandé)	15.59
Exterior Decor Group (not available with Mach I or Grandé)	32.44
Handling suspension (not available with Grandé or 200-, 250-, and 428-ci engines)	30.64
High-back bucket seats (not available with Grandé)	84.25
Interior Decor Group (not available with Mach I or Grandé)	101.10
Interior Decor Group with dual racing mirrors option	88.15
Intermittent windshield wipers	16.85
Four-speed manual transmission (302- and 351-ci V-8s)	204.64
Four-speed manual transmission with 390- and 428-ci V-8s	253.92
Full-width seat (hardtop; not available with console)	32.44
GT Equipment Group (not available with Grandé, six-cylinder, or 302-ci V-8 engines)	146.71
Limited-slip differential (with 250- and 302-ci V-8)	41.60
Mach I over 351-ci 2V	25.91
Mach I over 351-ci 2V V-8	99.74
Mach I over 351-ci 2V V-8	357.46
Mach I over 351-ci 2V V-8	224.12
Power convertible top	52.95
Power disc brakes (not available with 200-ci Six)	64.77
Power steering	94.95
Power ventilation (not available with SelectAire)	40.02
Pushbutton AM radio	61.40
Rear seat deck (SportsRoof and Mach I)	97.21
Rear seat speaker (hardtop and Grandé)	12.95
Remote-control outside mirror (left-hand side)	12.95
Rim-Blow deluxe steering wheel	35.70
SelectAire air conditioner (not available with 200- or 428-ci with four-speed manual transmission)	379.57
SelectShift transmission with 302- and 351-ci V-8s	200.85
SelectShift transmission with 390- and 428-ci V-8s	222.08
SelectShift transmission with six-cylinder engine	191.13
Speed control (with V-8 and SelectShift)	73.83
Stereo-Sonic tape system (AM radio required)	133.84
Tachometer (V-8 only)	54.45
Tilt-away steering wheel	66.14
Tinted windshield and windows	32.44
Traction-lock differential (not available with six-cylinders or 302 V-8)	63.51
Vinyl-covered roof (hardtop and Grandé)	84.25
Wheel covers (not available with Mach I, GT, or Grandé; standard on Exterior Decor Group)	21.38
Wire wheel covers (standard on Grandé; not available with Mach I or GT Group)	79.51
Wire wheel covers with Exterior Decor Group Option	58.27

The chrome-plated styled steel wheel and hubcap was standard on the Mach 1 and was optional on all other models except the Grandé.

five NACA scoops. All four brakes were cooled by ducts and scoops in the fenders and quarter panels. The two original GT350 and GT500 models remained. The KR designation was no longer necessary because the 428 Cobra Jet engine was standard in the GT500. The convertible was offered once more for 1969 in the GT350 and GT500 formats.

In addition to the wild new grille, nose, and hood work, the front fenders were completely fiberglass and had been designed to accommodate the huge air ducts. Wide body side stripes ran down the middle of the car's entire length. The stock Mustang SportsRoof's nonfunctional rear quarter-panel scoop was replaced by a bolt on Shelby scoop. The taillights were from a 1965

Taillights from a 1965 Thunderbird barely look recognizable on a Mustang! *"Fast" Eddie Stokes*

ABOVE: This 1969 Shelby GT500 packs the 335-horsepower 428 Cobra Jet engine. *"Fast" Eddie Stokes* BELOW: This is pure 428 Cobra Jet power! *"Fast" Eddie Stokes*

Thunderbird like the 1968 model. A massive aluminum exhaust outlet replaced the stock Mustang's license plate mounting bracket on the rear valance panel. No wonder this car didn't resemble a Mustang any more!

Interior

The Shelby's interior for 1969 received the Deluxe Interior Decor Group. The speedometer was a 140-mile-per-hour unit, and the tach was the standard 8,000-rpm model. The center console base was the same as the stock Mustang's except it utilized a new top housing for gauges and had a set of toggle switches for driving lights and courtesy lights, an ashtray, and a set of seat belt holsters. Both the SportsRoof and convertible models were equipped with a roll bar. Fold-down rear seats were standard on SportsRoof models.

Engines

The Shelby Cobra GT350 utilized the 290-horsepower 351 Windsor engine. It was Shelby-ized with a modified aluminum high-rise intake manifold and finned aluminum Cobra "Powered by Ford" valve covers. The Shelby Cobra GT500s packed 335-horsepower 428 Cobra Jet engines that featured a medium-rise aluminum intake and die-cast "428 Cobra Jet" valve covers.

Chapter 5

1970

Can you spot the differences between a 1969 and a 1970 Mustang? It's nowhere near as tough as the 1967–1968 comparison, even for the rank amateur. Although the two years shared the same body design, the "at first glance" differences were pretty significant. Major revisions included the front end, with its two-headlight configuration instead of the previous four; the simulated air scoops on either side of the grille; the lack of side scoops on the quarter panels, which had been a Mustang tradition; and the new taillight and taillight panel. Hero models, such as the Mach 1 and Boss 302, received radically different striping and graphics packages from their 1969 brethren.

The year 1970 saw the discontinuation of the GT Equipment Group and the continuation of

mustang '70

The iconic Boss 302 on the move! This Grabber Blue (J9) with White interior is definitely striking. This car was photographed on a twisting section of the Oregon coast.

Check out the cover of the retail sales brochure for 1970. It is sultry and minimalist.

the Grandé, Mach 1, Boss 302, and Boss 429 cars. Of course, the base hardtop, sexy SportsRoof, and classic convertible all made reappearances. The discontinuation of the 390 four-barrel engine, which was axed from the Mustang line after three years of faithful duty, and the addition of a new Cleveland four-barrel 351 also happened in 1970.

The ad and sales brochure campaigns for 1970 were simply the best! Sell lines were used that would never be considered politically correct in this day and age. Check out some of the verbiage from this 1970 retail sales brochure:

"Carol Edmonston had a B.A., M.A., and Ph.D., but really wanted her Mrs. Since she bought Mustang, she can't decide between Mr. B.A., Mr. M.A. or the Ph.D. Carol has decision problems, but nice ones. How about you? How about Mus-

1970
Performance
Buyer's Digest

The cars...The engines...The parts...Ford has everything you need for your kind of performance driving.

Ford put out a Performance Buyer's Digest for all its muscle in 1970. The two Mustangs Ford focused on were the Boss 302 and Mach 1. The brochure only used illustrations, as opposed to photography. Classic 1970s art!

tang Grandé? A formally dressed up model that includes a Landau-style roof in black or white grain vinyl; wood-tone accented instrument panel; locking, deluxe two-spoke steering wheel; and high-back, foam-filled bucket seats designed to wrap you cozily in uncommon comfort."

Or how about this advertising for the SportsRoof?

"Marc Muccino's coaching career was a big 'zero' until he bought his Mustang SportsRoof. Now it's a whole new ball game. Just like our friend Marc, watch the 'zeros' turn into 'ooohs'

when you hop behind the wheel of a Mustang SportsRoof. Its sleek silhouette has a roofline that slopes all the way back to a superstyled rear deck with a perky spoiler flip. Distinctive three-lens taillights will tell everyone to notice they've just been passed. Note the ventless curved side glass windows, the pop-open rear quarter window that introduces you to 'quiet' open window ventilation. A sporty energy-absorbing two-spoke steering wheel, padded energy-absorbing instrument panel, standard high-back bucket seats."

Boss 302 – Son of Trans – Am.

The Mustang Boss 302 is what comes from winning those Trans-Am championships. From its 5-litre, F.I.A. sanctioned V-8 to its 16-to-1 steering, the Boss is designed to go quick and hang tight. The standard specs sound like a $9,000 European sports job instead of a reasonably priced, reliable American pony car. Boss 302 comes in just one body style— the wind-splitting SportsRoof shape. The engine is Ford's high output 302 CID 4V V-8, with new cylinder heads to permit canting the valves for better gas flow and larger diameter—2.18 intake, 1.71 exhaust. That's what gives you a big 290 horsepower from a small, lightweight 302 CID engine.

Choose either close or wide ratios on Boss 302's butter-smooth, fully synchronized 4-speed. We've made it an even quicker box by adding a T-handle Hurst Shifter.*

Brakes are power boosted, ventilated floating caliper front discs. When we tell you the suspension is competition type with staggered rear shocks to combat rear wheel hop on take-off, don't take our word for it, give it a try. We glue the Boss to the road on 15-inch wheels with hub cap trim rings, shod with F60 x 15 superwide fiberglass belted bias-ply tires. All this standard equipment leaves you little to option but the fun things—like Magnum 500 chrome wheels, and those great Sport Slats for the tinted backlite. That's Boss 302. Your only problem . . . deciding whether to drive it or "Trans-Am" it.

Two Trans-Am Championships for Mustang taught us how to set up Boss 302.

Engine: 302 CID 4V V-8. (See page 16 for detailed engine specifications.) **Transmission:** 4-speed fully synchronized with Hurst Shifter®; standard wide ratios: 2.78:1, 1.93:1, 1.36:1, 1.0:1, optional close ratios 2.32:1, 1.69:1, 1.29:1, 1.0:1.

Rear Axle: Heavy-duty, 9" ring gear, standard ratio 3.50:1.

Brakes: Power-boosted floating caliper ventilated front disc brakes diameter 11.3", rear brakes 10" drums. Swept area 282.5 sq. in.

Wheelbase: 108". Overall length 187.4", tread, front and rear 59.5".

Suspension: Extra heavy-duty front coil and rear leaf springs, extra heavy-duty shock absorbers and front stabilizer bar, staggered rear shock absorbers, rear stabilizer bar.

Steering: Ratios, **Standard**—16:1 manual, **Optional**—16:1 power.

Wheels: 7" rims, F60 x 15 fiberglass belted tires with white lettering.

Details: Front spoiler standard, unique, "hockey stick" striping, matte black hood, high-back bucket seats, carpeting, aluminum valve covers. Collapsible, space saver spare tire.

Colors: Grabber Blue, Grabber Green, Grabber Orange. Plus 8 other colors.

Options: Special 3.50 or 3.91 Traction-Lok rear axle. Rear deck spoiler. Sport Slats louvers to cover backlite. Power steering. Magnum 500 chrome wheels. AM or AM/FM Stereo Radio. 8000-rpm tachometer, console. Knitted vinyl trim. (Note air conditioning is not available on Boss 302.)

Car and Driver Magazine says: "The Boss 302 . . . may just be the new standard by which everything from Detroit must be judged."

Paint a number on your Boss 302, put a big gas tank in it, and call yourself Parnelli Jones.

Mach 1 – quickest pony of them all!

Mach I. Just one model—the fastback with built-in spoiler. You don't need any more, and neither did Mickey Thompson when he boomed the prototype across the endless Bonne-ville Salt Flats to shatter an armload of Class B and C records.

Obviously the big hit with the Mustang Mach I has always been the great choice of power, and that's just the way we're going to keep things. To start off, there's the standard 351 2V job . . . and for street work it's a bushy-tailed mill indeed. Then come the options. Exhibit A: one brand-new 351 4V V-8. This is the one with the "Cleveland" heads. It has huge (2.19") intakes, 1.71" exhausts), canted valves and a walloping 11.0:1 compression ratio. Power? Three hundred big, strong, born-and-bred-in-America horses.

Not bad for the first option . . . right? Next is the 428 4V Cobra. This puts 440 foot-pounds of torque where it will do the most good. If you really want to move out quick, you can have your Mach I with a 428 Cobra Jet. This giant jewel of an engine features the functional "Shaker" hood scoop. It shakes and so does the competition. Nice thing about the people who build the Mach I . . . they don't do half the job and then lay down their tools. No matter which engine you pick—and we know it's a tough decision—you get the com-petition suspension. This includes extra heavy-duty front and rear springs, extra heavy-duty shock absorbers, and front and rear stabilizer bars. Also you get fiberglass belted tires. All the power you need, plus a suspension that lets you get it to the road. That's what makes the Mach I a complete package. And for '70, the Mach I looks as good as it goes. There's a unique black grille with driving lamps, black or white hood paint, wide aluminum rocker panel trim, high-back buckets in knitted vinyl, full instrumentation, woodtoned applique on panel and console, sweep-hand electric clock, and more. Get yourself a Mach I 428 and really "shake up" the troops.

From its Cobra Jet 428 Shaker scoop to lowered Sport Slats option and supertires, Mach I is Number One!

Wheels: 14", 7" rim, F70 x 14 wide tread, fiberglass belted bias-ply white sidewall tires (raised white letters with 428 CJ). **Suspension:** Com-petition type with front and rear stabilizer bar and extra heavy-duty springs, front shocks and rear shocks.

Details: Dual racing mirrors, high-back knitted vinyl bucket seats, console, sound package, three-spoke Rim-Blow woodtoned steering wheel, woodtoned appliques on instrument panel with clock, dual hood lock pins, rocker panel molding, honeycomb black panel applique, deck lid tape stripe, painted hood stripes, sports wheel covers, hood scoop (functional "Shaker" hood scoop on 428 4V Cobra Jet Ram-Air engine, optional with 351 2V and 4V V-8), unique grille with simulated driving lamps, pop-open gas cap, bright dual exhaust extensions with 351 4V and 428 4V engines.

Colors: Grabber Green, Grabber Blue, Grabber Orange, plus 13 other colors.

Mach 1 Options: Power Steering, AM or AM/FM Stereo Radio. Drag Pack (with 428 Cobra V-8), including Traction-Lok dif-ferential with 3.91 or 4.30 No-Spin differential, plus modified oil cooler, modified cap screw connecting rods, camshaft flywheel and damper. Quick ratio (16:1) manual steering, rear spoiler, sport slats for backlite. Tilt steering wheel, and much more.

Put one of these under your local Christmas Tree. Specially prepared Mach I drags in Super Stock— wins in Super Stock.

Engines: Standard—351 CID 2V V-8. **Optional**—351 4V V-8, 428 Cobra 4V V-8, 428 Cobra Jet 4V Ram-Air V-8. (See page 16 for detailed engine specifications.) **Transmissions: Stan-dard**—3-speed fully synchronized manual, ratios 2.42:1, 1.61:1, 1.0:1. (3-speed not available with 428 CID V-8's.) **Optional**—4-speed fully synchronized manual with Hurst Shifter® (avail-able with all engines); wide ratios: 2.78:1, 1.93:1, 1.36:1, 1.0:1, close ratio 2.32:1, 1.69:1, 1.29:1, 1.0:1. (Note: 428 CID V-8's require close-ratio 4-speed.) SelectShift Cruise-O-Matic ratios 2.46:1, 1.46:1, 1.0:1. **Rear Axle:** Ratios: 3-speed manual, 2.75:1, 3.0, 3.25; 4-speed manual, 3.0, 3.25, 3.50 SelectShift, 2.75, 3.0, 3.25, 3.50, Traction-Lok, 3.0, 3.25, 3.50, 3.91 No-Spin (w/428 Cobra and CJ Ram-Air manual transmissions) 4:30. **Brakes:** 10-in. drums, lining area 173.3 sq. in. **Optional**—Floating Caliper, Front Power Disc Brakes, swept area 231.0 sq. in. **Wheelbase:** 108.0" Length 187.4". Tread, front and rear 58.5".

Boss 429. An earth-shaking combination of big-bore engine and Trans-Am body. Limited production job, coax your dealer!

Then there's the jargon for the Mach 1:

"Hubert Bailey, the accountant who couldn't keep his figures balanced. He got a Mach 1 and figures are no longer his problem. A hot Mach 1 solved Hubert's problem. A standard 351-cube 250-horsepower 2V V-8 engine and three-speed floor-mounted transmission performed the magic. Take a look at the unique front end, bold new grille and grille lamps . . . the sporty hood latches and new black hood treatment. White hood striping is available with black or dark green exterior colors. Notice the hefty, optional F70 belted bias-ply tires with raised white letters. E70s are Mach 1 standards."

Ford was really going after the whole "this car will turn you into a somebody" thing with these kinds of sales pitches. Overall, Mustang sales were down significantly for the 1970 model year and fell to 191,522 units. Camaro still didn't catch up to the Mustang. Chevy's pony car sales also fell off and 124,889 units were sold in 1970. What was happening to the market? For the most part, skyrocketing insurance premiums and rapidly escalating gas prices were the problem. The year 1970 pretty much marked the end of the muscle car era and big-block firepower. The handwriting was all over the wall.

Total 1970 Mustang production saw 191,522 units, of which 96,151 were hardtops; 87,551 were fastbacks; and 7,820 were convertibles. See table in Chapter 1 for complete individual model production listing.

Body, Models, and Exterior Trim

According to Ford's public relations blitz for the 1970 model year, "The 1970 Mustang has been designed to sustain the leadership position which it has enjoyed since introduction in 1964. The new Mustang is built to fill the needs of all buyers in the 'sporty-compact' segment . . . whether their motivation is Luxury, Sports/Performance, or Economy."

Once again, the hardtop took care of business by selling the lion's share of Mustangs with 96,151 units. The base price was $2,721. The base Sports-Roof checked in with a sticker of $2,771, which was $153 more than the previous year. The base convertible was priced at $3,025. The Mach 1 with its base 351 2V powerplant was priced at $3,271. Considering that the GT wasn't around that year, and Mach 1 pricing looked all the better.

ABOVE: The last of the breed: the big, bad Boss 429 for 1970.

RIGHT: A Boss 302 in White (M) with a shaker scoop option.
Doug Bennett

THIS PAGE & OPPOSITE TOP: The spectacular 1970 Mustang Mach 1 in Code M White.

The 351 engine call-out identifies the base engine for the Mach 1.

- Simulated air scoops with a single horizontal bar were incorporated into the front fender extensions.
- A wide C-pillar with bright backlight molding accented in black on hardtop models.
- Ventless front side windows improved appearance and increased driver/passenger visibility.
- Parking lights were recessed into an air slot in the front splash panel below a streamlined front bumper.
- New recessed taillights were larger, retaining the vertical theme of previous models.
- Convertible models featured a vinyl top in black or white.
- Extra padding under the top fabric along the upper side areas provided a smoother exterior appearance.

Grandé models featured a landau vinyl roof covered in black or white Levant vinyl, and a camera case–textured lower back panel appliqué.

Mach 1 models featured a special grille with unique driving lamps. A revised hood treatment featured a wide paint stripe down the center of the hood, either in a low-gloss black or white, and a thinner tape stripe surrounded the large stripe. The engine size was noted on each side of the standard nonfunctional hood scoop. The Shaker scoop was standard with the 428 Cobra Jet Ram Air engine option. Twist-type hood latches replaced the older pin-style latches. There

The Grandé came standard with the 200-ci six and was priced at $2,926 for 1970.

Exterior Styling and Features

The new Mustang's bodywork was totally revised in 1969, so the styling was mostly a carryover for the 1970 model year. The changes were:
- Single 7-inch headlights and a matte black, injection-molded plastic horizontal-design grille highlighted by the tri-color Mustang emblem mounted in the center position.

ABOVE & OPPOSITE: The 1970 Mustang SportsRoof looks street tough in Code A Black.

LEFT: The Mach 1 emblem for 1970 molded into the lower body side trim was perhaps the best looking of all the Mach 1s.

was a new aluminum rocker panel molding that was finned, painted black, and featured "Mach 1" lettering on the front fender. A wide tape stripe was applied to the edge of the deck lid with Mach 1 lettering centered on the spoiler lip. Other changes included a black honeycomb rear panel appliqué and sports wheel covers, which were a simulated mag-style wheel cover.

Boss 302 featured a new hood treatment for 1970. A wide, low-gloss black stripe stretched the length of the hood. Triple tape stripes ran on either side of the wide stripe, diverted parallel to the windshield, and stopped atop the fenders. Boss 302 lettering appeared near the top of the fenders and a hockey stick stripe continued downward and continued along the side of the car. Boss 302 graphics also featured a low-gloss black rear panel and taillight bezels.

Boss 429 exterior styling included the same hood scoop as the previous model, but for 1970

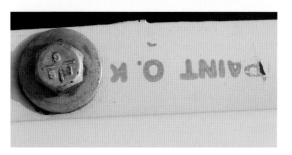

ABOVE: Mustang lettering had evolved over the years to a stylish script.

LEFT: The OK stamp was applied after the body passed the paint quality control section.

Headlights and parking lights illuminate at the same time. Simulated air scoops are barely noticeable on black Mustangs.

BODY SPECIFICATIONS

	Hardtop	Fastback	Convertible
Length (overall, inches)	187.4	187.46	187.4
Width (overall, inches)	71.3	71.3	71.3
Height (overall, inches)	51.2	51.2	51.2
Wheelbase (inches)	108	108	108
Curb weight (pounds)	2,875	2,899	2,985

(six cylinder, standard transmission)

VIN/TRIM/DSO TAG DECODING FOR 1970

Model Year Code
0= 1970

Assembly Plant Codes
F= Dearborn, Michigan   R= San Jose, California
T= Metuchen, New Jersey

Body Serial Codes
01= hardtop   02= fastback   03= convertible

Engine Codes
F= 302-ci eight-cylinder, 2 bbl   G= 302-ci eight-cylinder, 4 bbl (Boss 302)
H= 351-ci eight-cylinder, 2 bbl   L= 250-ci six-cylinder, 1 bbl
M= 351-ci eight-cylinder, 4 bbl   Q= 428-ci eight-cylinder, 4 bbl
R= 428-ci eight-cylinder, 4 bbl (Ram Air)
T= 200-ci six-cylinder, 1 bbl   Z= 429-ci eight-cylinder, 4 bbl (Boss 429)

Consecutive Number
The remaining six digits in the VIN indicate the vehicle's consecutive unit number assigned at the production line.

BODY STYLE CODES
63A fastback standard (bucket seat)
63B fastback Decor Group (bucket seat)
63C fastback standard (Mach 1)
65A hardtop standard (bucket seat)
65B hardtop Decor Group (bucket seat)
65E hardtop Grandé
76A convertible standard (bucket seat)
76B convertible Decor Group (bucket seat)

COLOR CODES
1= Vermillion	2= Light Ivy Yellow
6= Bright Blue Metallic	A= Black
C= Dark Ivy Green Metallic	D= Bright Yellow
G= Medium Lime Metallic	J9= Grabber Blue
K= Bright Gold Metallic	M= White
N= Pastel Blue	Q= Medium Blue Metallic
S= Medium Gold Metallic	T= Red
U9= Grabber Orange	Z9= Grabber Green

TRIM CODES

Hardtop, SportsRoof, Convertible (Bucket Seats, All Vinyl)
BA= Black   BB= Blue   BE= Vermillion   BF= Ginger   BG= Ivy   BW= White

Convertible (Optional Comfortweave Vinyl)
EA= Black   EB= Blue   EG= Ivy   EW= White

Hardtop, SportsRoof (Optional Comfortweave Vinyl)
TA= Black   TB= Blue   TG= Ivy   TW= White

Hardtop, SportsRoof (Blazer Stripe Cloth and Vinyl)
UE= Vermillion   UF= Ginger

Convertible (Blazer Stripe Cloth and Vinyl)
CE= Vermillion   CF= Ginger

Grandé Hardtop (Houndstooth Cloth and Vinyl)
AA= Black   AB= Blue   AE= Vermillion   AF= Ginger   AG= Ivy

Mach 1 SportsRoof (Comfortweave Vinyl)
3A= Black   3B= Blue   3E= Vermillion   3F= Ginger   3G= Ivy   3W= White

DATE CODES

The number (1–31) appearing before the month letter indicates the day.

Month	First Year	Second Year
January	A	N
February	B	P
March	C	Q
April	D	R
May	E	S
June	F	T
July	G	U
August	H	V
September	J	W
October	K	X
November	L	Y
December	M	Z

DSO CODES

This code indicates the city/area in which the vehicle was originally destined for delivery.

11= Boston, Massachusetts	13= New York City, New York
15= Newark, New Jersey	16= Philadelphia, Pennsylvania
17= Washington, D.C.	21= Atlanta, Georgia
22= Charlotte, North Carolina	24= Jacksonville, Florida
25= Richmond, Virginia	28= Louisville, Kentucky
32= Cleveland, Ohio	33= Detroit, Michigan
35= Lansing, Indiana	37= Buffalo, New York
38= Pittsburgh, Pennsylvania	41= Chicago, Illinois
43= Milwaukee, Wisconsin	44= Twin Cities, Minnesota
46= Indianapolis, Indiana	47= Cincinnati, Ohio
51= Denver, Colorado	
53= Kansas City, Missouri	
54= Omaha, Nebraska	
55= St. Louis, Missouri	
56= Davenport, Iowa	
61= Dallas, Texas	
62= Houston, Texas	
63= Memphis, Tennessee	
64= New Orleans, Louisiana	
65= Oklahoma City, Oklahoma	
71= Los Angeles, California	
72= San Jose, California	
73= Salt Lake City, Utah	
74= Seattle, Washington	
75= Phoenix, Arizona	
83= Government	
84= Home Office Reserve	
85= American Red Cross	
89= Transportation Services	
90–99= Export	

This Boss 429 featured its own chin spoiler. The car was originally equipped with the F60x15 tires.

The taillight style changed dramatically for 1970. Still retaining its three-bar design, some say this was the best-looking taillight ever on a Mustang.

The side marker lights were rectangular and were set into the body.

RIGHT: The twist-off gas cap was simple and elegant.

FAR RIGHT: Dual exhaust tips lurk beneath the rear valance panel.

AXLE CODES		
Conventional	Limited Slip	Axle Ratio
0		2.50
2	K	2.75
3		2.79
4	M	2.80
5		2.83
6	O	3.00
7		3.10
8		3.20
9	R	3.25
A	S	3.50
B		3.07
C		3.08
F	X	2.33
V		3.91
W		4.30

the scoop was black on all cars, regardless of exterior color.

The Decor Group ($78.00, $97 for convertibles) was primarily an interior upgrade package. Exterior highlights included dual racing mirrors color-keyed to the exterior and bright rocker panel and wheel lip moldings.

For the 1970 model year only, Ford offered a special striping package on the Mustang SportsRoof called the Grabber SportsRoof. It included a side tape graphic similar to the 1969 Boss 302 striping, 14-inch flat hubcaps, and trim rings. A second version of the Grabber SportsRoof featured a 1970 Boss 302-type side stripe treatment with either a 302 or 351 designator at the top of the stripe directly underneath the side mirrors.

Interior

With an interior design that was very close to the 1969 model year, the hoopla was kept to a dull roar for 1970. The high-back bucket seats that were optional on the 1969s were now standard on the 1970 models. The standard steering wheel design changed, as did the column design. For the first time in Mustang history, the ignition lock cylinder was located on the column instead of the instrument panel.

The changes included:
- Double hood instrument panel and standard high-back bucket seats were standard.

1970 STANDARD EQUIPMENT

- Accelerator pedal: suspended type
- Alternator: 45 amps
- Arm rests: front
- Ashtray: front
- Backup lights
- Battery: Autolite Sta-Ful design, 45 amps
- Body: rust resistant and insulated
- Bodyside paint stripes (Grandé only)
- Brakes: self adjusting
- Bucket seats: High back, foam padded, adjustable
- Carpets: 100 percent nylon, molded, color-keyed
- Choke: automatic
- Cigarette lighter
- Coolant: two years or 36,000 miles
- Courtesy lights: door switches
- Curved side glass
- Door checks: two stages
- Door hinges: bronze, bushed
- Door trim: all vinyl
- Electric clock: Grandé and Mach 1 only
- Emergency flashers: eight ways
- Engine: 200 Six (except Mach 1)
- Engine: 302 (Boss 302 only)
- Engine: 351 (Mach 1 only)
- Exhaust emission control system: all engines
- Finish: Super Diamond Lustre Enamel
- Front fenders: bolt-on
- Fuel tank: 22 gallons (20 gallons on California units)
- Glass: safety laminated windshield
- Glass: safety, solid tempered, side and rear
- Glass: tinted backlight (SportsRoof only)
- Glove box: instrument panel mounted
- Headlights: single
- Headlining: color-keyed vinyl
- Heater and defroster: fresh air
- Hood latch: single action
- Hubcaps: stainless steel (except Grandé and Mach 1)
- Jack: scissors type
- Keyless locking
- Lamps, bulbs: extended life
- Landau vinyl roof (Grandé only)
- Lubrication, chassis: 36,000 miles or 36 months
- Mirror: outside rearview, left-hand side
- Molding: rocker panel (Grandé and Mach 1 only)
- Molding: wheel lip (Grandé only)
- Muffler: aluminized and stainless steel
- Reversible keys
- Scuff plates: aluminum
- Thermostat: 195 degrees Fahrenheit
- Tires: fiberglass belted, bias-ply
- Transmission: three-speed manual
- Transmission lever: tunnel mounted
- Unilock safety harness
- Upholstery: all vinyl
- Upholstery: cloth and vinyl (Grandé only)
- Upholstery: Comfortweave knitted vinyl (Mach 1 only)
- Valve lifters: hydraulic (except Boss 302)
- Ventilation: Flow-Thru
- Ventless side glass
- Windshield washers
- Windshield wipers: two-speed electric

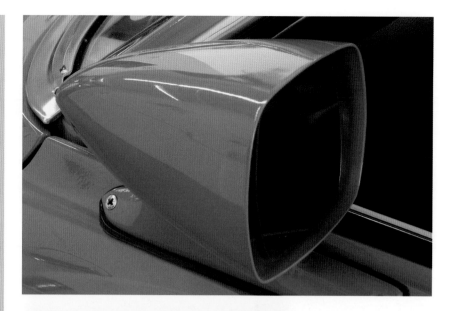

TOP: The Mach 1, Boss 302, and Boss 429 all came standard with color-keyed racing mirrors.

LEFT: The Boss 429 lettering decal was subdued, and was affixed to the fenders. It was very understated, compared to the wild Mach 1 and Boss 302 graphics.

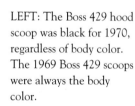

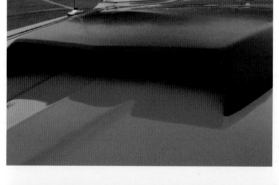

LEFT: The Boss 429 hood scoop was black for 1970, regardless of body color. The 1969 Boss 429 scoops were always the body color.

BELOW: The 1970 Mach 1 featured a honeycomb-textured black back panel. *Doug Bennett*

TOP: The 1970 Mach 1 interior, like the 1969, included many options from the Decor Group.

RIGHT: Inside this mighty Boss 429 the seats are White with Comfortweave option. All bucket seats for 1970 were now the high-back style.

- Unilock, three-point safety harnesses were standard for the driver and front seat passenger.
- Squeeze-type door handles were recessed in the padded energy-absorbing armrests.
- All-vinyl interior was available in Black, White, Blue, Vermillion, Ivy Green, or Ginger.
- Nylon carpeting was color-keyed to the interior.

Grandé's interior included houndstooth cloth and vinyl seat trim on the high-back bucket seats, simulated teakwood grained instrument panel and cluster appliqué, deluxe two-spoke steering wheel that included simulated teakwood trim,

The seatbelt was brushed metal with an irregular-shaped pushbutton release.

molded door panels with courtesy lights, electric clock with sweep second hand, and bright trimmed pedal pads.

Mach 1's interior featured high-back bucket seats with Comfortweave knitted vinyl inserts; a deluxe three-spoke rim-blow steering wheel; color-keyed carpeting; a floor console; simulated woodgrain trim on the console, instrument panel, and door panels; molded door trim panels with courtesy lamps; an electric clock; and bright-trimmed pedal pads.

The all-new-for-1969 instrument panel stayed the same for 1970. The driver directly faced the four large pods that were deep set in the instrument panel. The pods were set in a black camera case plastic housing. The two inner pods were larger in diameter than the two outer pods. Left to right, the pods contained the alternator, speedometer, fuel/coolant, and oil pressure gauges. Arrow-shaped turn indicator lights were located in the outer smaller pods.

TOP: The Decor Group interior for 1970 from a SportsRoof Mustang.

ABOVE: The door panels for 1970 were the molded type. This is from a Boss 429 that includes Decor Group interior accoutrements.

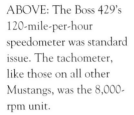

ABOVE: The Boss 429's 120-mile-per-hour speedometer was standard issue. The tachometer, like those on all other Mustangs, was the 8,000-rpm unit.

LEFT: The rim-blow steering wheel activated the horn when the rim was squeezed.

TOP: While the 1969 Mach 1s featured a red band on the seat backs, the 1970 models used a charcoal gray motif.
ABOVE: Optional Comfortweave seats are shown in a standard SportsRoof. High back bucket seats were now standard equipment.

ABOVE: The standard pushbutton AM radio in the Deluxe interior. BELOW: The optional AM/FM radio for 1970 was a premium stereo unit. It is shown here with the Decor Group.

For 1970, the luxury interior package was referred to as the Decor Group. The MSRP was $78.00 ($97.00 on convertible) and included:

- Choice of high-back bucket seat in Comfortweave or the new Blazer Stripe (see interior trim options in the VIN/Trim/DSO tag decoding for 1970 chart)
- Simulated woodgrain instrument panel appliqués that included M-U-S-T-A-N-G labeling on the passenger side
- Instrument panel gauges of dark gray instead of black
- Speedometer marked in increments of five
- Deluxe two-spoke steering wheel with added woodgrain trim
- One-piece deluxe molded door panels with woodgrain appliqué and carpeted lower sections

Neither of these packages was available for the Grandé or Mach 1 since both models included decor items as standard equipment. All Mustang optional interiors were available for the Boss 302 for 1970. Boss 429s came standard with the Interior Decor Group.

Other popular interior options included: an 8,000-rpm tachometer (with the standard interior tachometer face being black with white numbers, while the Decor Group featured gray-faced tach), AM radio, AM/FM radio, AM/eight-track tape combination, bench seat, console, Convenience Group, two electric clock models, Select-Aire air conditioning, intermittent windshield wipers, deluxe seat belts with reminder light, tilt-away steering wheel, rim-blow three-spoke steering wheel, and speed control. For a complete listing of all options, see options chart in this chapter.

Chassis

As described in Chapter 1, "the platform carries the body on the top, encloses the engine, and provides attaching points for the various chassis components. It also provides the basic structure of the car. The platform is made up of a box-section front and rear side rails tied in securely to heavy boxed-in rocker panels. These components are connected by five heavy gauge crossmembers to form an extra strong ladder-type framing under the car. The front and rear side rails extend partially under, and are welded

TOP: A Boss 302 with nonshaker induction. Valve covers were natural finish magnesium for 1970. ABOVE: A Mach 1 with the 428 CJ engine with shaker scoop. The engine displacement callout was in the hood graphic.

A Boss 302 with shaker scoop. The scoop was attached directly to the top of the air cleaner and helped with the induction of fresh air. It probably didn't add any horsepower, but it sure looked cool!

to, the floor pan. The full-depth, full-length tunnel down the center of the floor pan adds a backbone to give the structure maximum rigidity. The full-depth side panels in the engine compartment are welded to the front side rails at the bottom and to the cowl at the rear. The tops of these panels are pressed over to form a wide flange and increase front end rigidity. A one-piece stamping with a deep channel section at the top connects the inside panels across the front."

Regardless of the car's engine size, all Mustangs were based on the same platform chassis. Upgraded suspension components compensated for the weight differences in engines.

Engines

200-ci Six

The 200-ci six remained standard on all Mustang models for 1970.

Quick facts:
- Seven main bearings: smoother engine operation, less vibration, longer engine life
- Hydraulic valve lifters: quiet operation, low maintenance
- Large valves: more efficient breathing, more seat area for better cooling and less burning
- Short stroke design: less vibration, less wear
- Single-venturi carburetor: economical operation

BASE EQUIPMENT ENGINE: T-CODE

- Bore and stroke: 3.68x3.13
- Carburetor: Autolite 1100, 1V
- Compression ratio: 8.7:1
- Displacement: 200 ci
- Horsepower: 120 at 4,000 rpm
- Torque: 190 ft-lbs at 2,200 rpm
- Type: inline six-cylinder, overhead valve
- Valve lifters: hydraulic

OPTIONAL EQUIPMENT ENGINE: L-CODE

- Bore and stroke: 3.68x3.91
- Carburetor: Autolite 1100, 1V
- Compression ratio: 9.0:1
- Displacement: 250 ci
- Horsepower: 155 at 4,400 rpm
- Torque: 240 ft-lbs at 1,600 rpm
- Type: inline six-cylinder, overhead valve
- Valve lifters: hydraulic

- Six-month or 6,000-mile oil filter: reduced maintenance, improved oil filtering
- Automatic choke: sensed ambient and coolant temperatures, helped prevent flooding on semiwarm starts
- Compression ratio of 8.7:1: better efficiency on regular or economy gasoline
- Thin wall casting: better cooling, less weight
- Precision-molded crankshaft: dependable, smooth operation
- Weather-insulated ignition system: reliable starts under all climatic conditions

250-ci Six

The Big Six 250-ci engine continued on in 1970 as the optional six-cylinder engine for Mustang. The 250 was standard in the Fairlane and optional in the Mustang.

Quick facts (highlights):

- Designed for emission control: design resulted in a more effective combustion process than added-on emission control equipment found in comparable engines in the 250-ci range
- Nearly square bore-to-stroke dimensions: the 3.68 to 3.91 ratio resulted in a compact combustion chamber configuration that

efficiently utilized the fuel and reduced exhaust emission

- Closed crankcase ventilation: designed for efficient reburning of combustion gases; had a closed, recirculating circuit that prevented the escape of fumes or combustion gases from the engine crankcase
- Hot and cold air cleaner system: sensed its own intake air temperature needs and selected manifold-heated air or air direct from outside; resulted in efficient fuel combustion and economy, improved performance, and virtual elimination of stalls due to carburetor icing; more precise calibration of the carburetor was achieved because the narrow range of incoming air temperature
- Controlled automatic choke: choke operation

OPTIONAL EQUIPMENT ENGINE: F-CODE

- Bore and stroke: 4.00x3.00
- Carburetor: Ford 2100 (290 cfm), 2V
- Compression ratio: 9.5:1
- Displacement: 302 ci
- Horsepower: 220 at 4,600 rpm
- Torque: 300 ft-lbs at 2,600 rpm
- Type: eight cylinder, overhead valve
- Valve lifters: hydraulic

Boss 429: the king of the beasts. A high-lift mechanical lifter camshaft was in full production for 1970.

This is the base engine for Mach 1 in 1970: the 351 two-barrel V-8. The engine is very common except for the fact that this one was ordered with a shaker scoop. This engine is an extremely low mileage original.

was automatically controlled by both engine temperature and vacuum conditions to utilize exhaust heat and improve starting and cold driveaway performance
- Larger water pump bearings: the bearing size increased to ¼-inch diameter for improved durability and operation

302-ci V-8 2V

The 302-ci two-barrel V-8 continued on into the 1970 Mustangs.

Quick facts:
- Molded crankshaft: extra engine stability, smoother operating
- Connecting rods and pistons: short connecting rods with extra strength design, deep skirt pistons with tolerance for longer engine wear
- Hot and cold dual inlet cleaner system: reduced throttle plate icing in cold weather, and improved engine operation required for emission control
- Full-length, full-circle water jackets: uniform cylinder temperature with a minimum of hot spots
- High capacity fuel filter: inline design to provide maximum filtration
- Hydraulic valve lifters: no adjustment required
- Dual advance distributor: correct spark advance for all driving conditions
- Six-month or 6,000-mile oil filter: reduced maintenance, improved oil filtering

---

OPTIONAL EQUIPMENT ENGINE: H-CODE (CLEVELAND AND WINDSOR)

- Bore and stroke: 4.00x3.50
- Carburetor: Ford 2100 (350 cfm), 2V
- Compression ratio: 9.5:1
- Displacement: 351 ci
- Horsepower: 250 at 4,600 rpm
- Torque: 355 ft-lbs at 2,600 rpm
- Type: eight cylinder, overhead valve
- Valve lifters: hydraulic

OPTIONAL EQUIPMENT ENGINE: M-CODE (CLEVELAND)

- Bore and stroke: 4.0x3.5
- Carburetor: (600 cfm), 4V
- Compression ratio: 11.0:1
- Displacement: 351 ci
- Horsepower: 300 at 5,400 rpm
- Torque: 380 ft-lbs at 3,400 rpm
- Type: eight cylinder, overhead valve
- Valve lifters: hydraulic

- Lightweight cast-iron construction: advanced thin wall castings

351-ci V-8 2V and 4V

The 351 was available for 1970 Mustangs, both in two- and four-barrel versions. The two-barrel version (H-code) production was done at the Windsor and Cleveland plants, while the four-barrel 351 was a brand-new design and built in Cleveland. Ford's ad copy of the day read: "The 351-ci 4V is a completely new engine design related to the 429 series and to the 302 Boss. This is a deep breathing engine characterized by canted large valves, rounded ports, and exceptionally sturdy main bearing caps."

Four-barrel

The cylinder blocks were a new precision-cast thin wall design that featured an integral timing chain chamber and integral water crossover passage in front of the block. Exceptionally wide main bearing caps and ½-inch bolts supported the new 2¾-inch crankshaft bearings. The deeper block and broader bearing support provided excellent durability and stability.

The cylinder heads were broader and patterned after the 429-ci canted valve head. The heads had larger, more efficient ports and larger valves (2.19-inch diameter intake and 1.71-inch exhaust). In addition to their large size, the valves were canted to favor maximum flow capacity. The exhaust valves were positioned toward the outboard side of the cylinder head for a more gradual directional change and unrestricted cross-section in the exhaust port. In addition, the length of the high-temperature port area exposed to the engine coolant was minimized.

The crankshaft was a new design with 2¾-inch main bearing, the carburetor was a 600-cfm capacity unit designed for the engine, and the exhaust manifold was a free-flowing header type.

428-ci V-8 4V (Ram Air and non-Ram Air)

The 428 Cobra Jet engine, first introduced in the 1968 Mustang, continued on into 1970 both as Ram Air and non–Ram Air versions. Non–Ram Air versions were designated Q-codes and fitted with a standard snorkel-type air cleaner. The Ram Air version was equipped with an air cleaner assembly with a vacuum-actuated bypass inlet valve mounted in the top.
Quick facts:

- Full-length, full-circle water jackets: designed to take advantage of thin wall casting; permitted higher overall engine operating temperature for increased performance capabilities
- New exhaust header-type manifolds: larger

OPTIONAL EQUIPMENT ENGINE: Q-CODE (NON-RAM AIR)

- Bore and stroke: 4.13x3.98
- Carburetor: Holley 4150 (735 cfm), 4V
- Compression ratio: 10.6:1
- Displacement: 428 ci
- Horsepower: 335 at 5,200 rpm
- Torque: 445 ft-lbs at 3,400 rpm
- Type: eight cylinder, overhead valve
- Valve lifters: hydraulic

OPTIONAL EQUIPMENT ENGINE: R-CODE (RAM AIR)

- Bore and stroke: 4.13x3.98
- Carburetor: Holley 4150 (735 cfm), 4V
- Compression ratio: 10.6:1
- Displacement: 428 ci
- Horsepower: 335 at 5,200 rpm
- Torque: 445 ft-lbs at 3,400 rpm
- Type: eight cylinder, overhead valve
- Valve lifters: hydraulic

inside dimensions and extended runner lengths blended into a larger collection chamber and aided in the extraction of exhaust gases, especially in the high-rpm capabilities of the 428s

- Electronically balanced crankshaft: a vibration damper, floated and mounted on rubber, on the front end of the crankshaft counteracted torsional vibration and provided smoother operation
- Heavy-duty valve springs: allowed engine to exceed 5,000 rpm without encountering valve float
- Special high lift camshaft: stepped bearings reduced any possibility of damage during assembly; cam lobes were precision ground to provide maximum power at high rpm
- Dual advance distributor: correct spark advance was maintained for all driving conditions, centrifugal advance and vacuum-controlled advance permitted more precise distributor calibration for a more efficient engine operation
- Full flow fuel filter: maximum filtration was provided with minimum restriction for higher efficiency and power output

OPTIONAL EQUIPMENT ENGINE: G-CODE (BOSS 302)

- Bore and stroke: 4.00x3.00
- Carburetor: Holley 4150 (780 cfm) 4V
- Compression ratio: 10.6:1
- Displacement: 302 ci
- Horsepower: 290 at 5,800 rpm
- Torque: 290 ft-lbs at 4,300 rpm
- Type: eight cylinder, overhead valve
- Valve lifters: solid

The thermactor air bypass valve is part of the vehicle's emission controls. All Ford engines utilized this system.

Continuing on into the 1970 model year, the Super Cobra Jet engine was installed if the Drag Pack option was ordered. The Drag Pack option consisted of either the V-code (3.91:1) or W-code (4.30:1) axle ratios. For a full description of this engine, see the engine section in Chapter 4 (1969).

302-ci V-8 4V (Boss 302)

The high-winding Boss 302 engine continued into the 1970 model year. The engine was available only in the Boss 302 Mustang SportsRoof model.

Quick facts (highlights):
- Cylinder heads: broader to accommodate the canted valves and splayed rocker arms; canted valves improved the gas flow, allowed larger-diameter valves, and provided room between the pushrods for improved

An optional automatic transmission was offered with the 1970 Mach 1. Note the Decor Group trim.

OPTIONAL EQUIPMENT ENGINE: Z-CODE (BOSS 429)
• Bore and stroke: 4.36x3.59
• Carburetor: Holley 4150 (780 cfm), 4V
• Compression ratio: 10.5:1
• Displacement: 429 ci
• Horsepower: 375 at 5,200 rpm
• Torque: 450 ft-lbs at 3,400 rpm
• Type: eight cylinder, overhead valve
• Valve lifters: solid (on later "T" versions)

design, nearly round ports that were important to the swirling action of the gas at high velocity; large $\frac{7}{16}$-inch UBS head bolts were used to fasten the heads to the block for an extra margin of strength
- Forged crankshaft: specially balanced at higher than normal speeds to accommodate the capacity of this powerplant; four-bolt main bearing caps strengthened the foundation of this competition engine
- Connecting rods: heavy-duty with $\frac{3}{8}$-inch nut and bolt fasteners
- Intake manifold: aluminum free-flow design with large runners to match the cylinder heads
- Valve covers: natural finish magnesium

429-ci V-8 4V (Boss 429)

The big Boss 429 engine carried over into the 1970 model year with a few changes. Most notably, a high-lift mechanical lifter camshaft was now in full production, a 780-cfm Holley carb (as oppose to a 735-cfm used in 1969) was utilized, and the valve covers were a natural finish magnesium. Despite the large size of this engine, the use of lightweight alloys kept the weight down to that of substantially smaller units.

TRANSMISSION CODES
1= three-speed manual
5= four-speed manual wide-ratio
6= four-speed manual close-ratio
U= automatic (C6)
V= semiautomatic stick shift
W= automatic (C4)
X= automatic (FMX)
Z= automatic (C6 Special)

For further facts on the Boss 429, see the engine section in Chapter 4 (1969).

Transmissions

For 1970, Ford advertised the three-speed manual as standard on all Ford Division cars except the Thunderbird and models with Boss 302, 428-ci, 429-ci, or Boss 429 engines.

The four-speed manual transmission was optional with all engines except the 200-ci six-cylinder. The transmission was fully synchronized in all forward gears and permitted upshifts and downshifts at speed without gear clash or noise.

The SelectShift Cruise-O-Matic transmission was a fully automatic unit and was available as optional equipment in all Mustang models except Boss 302 and Boss 429. This transmission also permitted manual shifting.

Suspension, Steering, and Brakes

Front Suspension

The suspension on the 1970 model Mustangs was the same as the previous 1969 model. Ford sales literature touted the front suspension with, "Mustang uses a short and long arm ball joint front suspension. Springs and shocks are calibrated to match the weight/ride requirements of each application, depending on the car model, engine, and optional equipment."

Front suspension features included:
- Single lower drag strut stabilizer arm was mounted to the frame through rubber bushings to eliminate metal-to-metal contact and reduce the amount of vibration and noise transmitted to the passenger area.
- The drag strut was anchored in a rubber bushing that allowed the wheels to move slightly toward the rear when hitting a bump. This controlled rear movement absorbed part of the initial road shock before it reached the passenger area.
- A link-type stabilizer bar with rubber bushings connected the right- and left-hand lower suspension arms and prevented excessive lean when cornering.

Rear Suspension

Mustang's Hotchkiss-type rear suspension featured rubber bushings at connection points to prevent metal-to-metal contact and minimize noise transfer to the passenger compartment.

Features of the system included:
- Long 53-inch, multileaf springs smoothed out driving and braking forces to provide a comfortable, cushioned ride.

- Front spring mounting eye incorporated a large resilient rubber bushing that permitted slight horizontal wheel movement to help absorb small bumps and reduce road shock and noise.
- Rear spring shackle was rubber-bushed compression type, allowing easy flexing on light impact and providing greater resistance to severe impact.
- Shock absorbers were mounted at an angle to reduce side sway and improve control. A constant viscosity fluid was used to provide uniform performance under all climatic conditions.
- The competition suspension had a staggered shock arrangement designed to control spring windup and wheel hop. The left shock absorber was relocated to the rear of the axle, and the right shock stayed ahead of the axle.

Steering

The Mustang's manual steering system for 1970 models was described in Ford sales literature as: " . . . a parallelogram linkage type with a cross link and idler arm. This system offers more positive control of the car under all driving conditions with a minimum of steering effort. For 1970, an optional quick ratio (16:1) manual steering is available on all Mustang models."

Features of the manual steering system included:
- Cross link bar was positioned in a way to improve directional stability and reduce oversteer.
- Steering shaft control assembly was driven by recirculating ball bearings in a closed channel for reduced friction. The Magic-Circle steering gear was filled with a lifetime lubricant that didn't need changing under normal circumstances.

Rear suspension consisted of multileaf springs and shock absorbers. This system was used on all Mustangs from 1967 to 1970.

REGULAR PRODUCTION OPTIONS

250-ci 155-horsepower Six; extra charge over 200-ci Six	39.00
302-ci (2V) 220 horsepower V-8; extra charge over 200-ci Six	101.00
351-ci (2V) 250-horsepower V-8; extra charge over 302-ci V-8 (standard Mach I)	45.00
351-ci (4V) 300-horsepower V-8 (except Mach I); extra charge over 302-ci V-8	93.00
428-ci (4V) 335-horsepower Cobra V-8 (except Mach I); extra charge over 302-ci V-8	356.00
428-ci (4V) 335-horsepower Cobra Jet Ram Air V-8 (except Mach I)	421.00
Mach I over 351-ci 2V	48.00
Mach I over 351-ci 2V	376.00
Mach I over 351-ci V-8	311.00

Transmissions

Four-speed manual transmission (standard on Boss 302) with 302-, 351-, and 428-ci V-8s	205.00
SelectShift (not available with Boss 302) with 200- and 250-ci Sixes or 302 and 351 V-8s	201.00
SelectShift with 428-ci V-8s	222.00

Power Assists

Power front disc brakes (standard on Boss 302; not available with 200-ci Six)	65.00
Power steering	95.00

Comfort-Convenience Equipment

Air conditioner, SelectAire (not available with 200 ci, Boss 302, or 428 ci with four-speed manual transmission)	380.00
Belts, deluxe with reminder light	15.00
Clock, electric rectangular (not available with Grandé, Mach I, or Decor Group)	16.00
Clock, electric round (standard with Grandé and Mach I) with Decor Group only	16.00
Console (standard with Mach I)	54.00
Convenience Group with Grandé, Mach I, Boss 302, or models with Decor Group	32.00
All other models	45.00
Defogger, rear window (two-door hardtops only)	26.00
F70x14 WSW tires, or F70x14 BSW tires with white raised letters	7.00
Glass, tinted (complete)	32.00
Mirrors, color-keyed dual racing (standard with Grandé, Mach I, Boss 302, or models with Decor Group)	26.00
Seat, rear sport deck (SportsRoof, Mach I, and Boss 302 only)	97.00
Space saver spare (standard with Boss 302; not available with 200-ci Six) with E70x14,	
Space saver spare with E78x14 BSW tires	20.00
Space saver spare with E78x14 WSW tires	13.00
Steering wheel, Rim-Blow deluxe three-spoke (standard with Mach I)	39.00

Steering wheel, tilt	45.00
Windshield wipers, intermittent	26.00

Audio Options

Radio, AM	61.00
Radio, AM/FM	214.00
Stereo-Sonic tape system (AM radio required)	134.00

Appearance Options

Bumper guards, front	13.00
Convertibles	97.00
Decor Group (not available with Mach I or Grandé) with Boss 302 and models except convertibles	78.00
Hardtop	84.00
Molding, rocker panel (standard with Decor Group; not available with Grandé, Mach I, or Boss 302)	16.00
Paint stripes, dual accent (standard on Grandé; optional on Mach I only)	13.00
Roof, vinyl (hardtop and Grandé only)	26.00
Sports slats (required dual racing mirrors) SportsRoof models only	65.00
Trim rings/hubcaps (standard on Boss 302; not available on Grandé or Mach I)	26.00
Wheels, argent-style steel (standard on Mach I; not available with Boss 302 or 200 Six Grandé)	32.00
All other models	58.00
Wheel covers, sports (standard on Mach I; not available with 200 Six) with Grandé and Boss 302	32.00
Wheel covers (standard on Grandé; not available with Boss 302 or Mach I)	26.00
All other models	58.00
Wheels, Magnum 500 chrome (Boss 302 only)	129.00

Performance Options

Axle, drag pack (not available with Boss 302; optional only with 428-ci V-8s with 3.91x4.30 axle ratios)	155.00
Axle, optional radio	13.00
Axle, Traction-Lok differential	43.00
Battery, heavy-duty 55-amp (standard on 200 Six with SelectShift and 351-ci 2V); available only with 250 Six, 302-ci V-8, or with 351-ci 2V V-8 in combination with manual transmission	13.00
Battery, heavy-duty 70-amp (standard on 351-ci 4V); available only with 200-ci engine with SelectShift and 351-ci 2V V-8	13.00
Extra cooling package (standard on SelectAire and 428-ci V-8; not available with Boss 302)	13.00
Hood scoop, Shaker (standard on 428 Cobra Jet V-8) with Boss 302, 351 2V, or 4V V-8	65.00
Spoiler, rear deck (SportsRoof, Mach I, and Boss 302 only)	20.00
Steering, quick ratio (standard on Boss 302)	16.00
Suspension, competition (standard on Mach I, Boss 302, and 428-ci V-8s; not available with Sixes)	31.00
Tachometer and trip odometer (not available with Sixes)	54.00

Power Steering

Power steering was optional for all 1970 Mustang models. The system utilized the standard manual steering linkage with a 16:1 ratio and Ford's Better Idea Fluidic-Control power steering pump that supplied power when you needed it and coasted at high speeds. Functioning through a unique patented Fluidic-Control, the pump forced the maximum amount of fluid through the system at low speeds for parking or cornering. At highway speeds, it reduced the fluid flow to provide a "feel" of the road and save engine

horsepower. The cross link had a ball joint stud attachment that was integrated with the power cylinder assembly.

Features of the unit also included a built-in low restriction feature of the control valve that allowed the wheels to return to the center position after making a turn. A 20.5:1 overall steering ratio provided responsive steering and reduced steering effort.

Brakes

All Mustangs for 1970 were equipped with a dual

ABOVE: The dual reservoir master brake cylinder was used on all Mustangs from 1967 to 1970.

RIGHT: These front disc brakes from the Boss 429 were 11.3-inch rotors. Rear brakes were drum and 10 inches in diameter. The Boss 302's brakes had the same specifications.

hydraulic brake system. The standard brakes on all cars were a duo-servo design—self-energizing, single anchor, internal expanding, and air cooled. The linings were self-adjusting when the brakes were applied while the car was moving in reverse. Front wheel power disc brakes were optional on all V-8-powered Mustangs.

Heating and Ventilation

For 1970, Ford referred to its ventilation system as Flow-Thru ventilation: "All 1970 Mustang models incorporate the new 'Flow-Thru' fresh air ventilation system which provides a significant improvement in air flow through the vehicle with the windows rolled up and helps to eliminate traffic and wind noise. With this new system, ventilating air, heated or unheated, can now enter from the front intake, circulate throughout the interior, and exit into the trunk and out through the B-pillar, carrying away stale or smoke-laden air without any need to open a window. The pressure relief valve has a one-way design to prevent reverse flow of air when the system is not in use."

The SelectAire air conditioner was an option for 1970, with an MSRP of $380. As stated on the RPO list, SelectAire was not available for Mustangs equipped with the 200-ci six, Boss 302 package, or the 428-ci engine with four-speed manual transmissions.

Wheels and Tires

The standard 1970 Mustang wheel was a 14x5-inch stamped steel unit with vent holes. Mustangs

equipped with a six-cylinder engine had wheels with a four-lug bolt pattern. The standard tire was E78x14. The standard wheel cover was a 10½-inch hubcap with the words "FORD MOTOR COMPANY" stamped in a circular pattern in the center. Most 1970 Mustangs were equipped with a full wheel cover that featured 16 simulated air slots. Boss 302 and Boss 429 Mustangs came with

The front suspension consisted of upper A-arm and lower stabilizer arm configuration. The spring is a coil-over-shock setup. This basic system was used on all Mustangs from 1967 to 1970.

F60x15 superwide oval tires mounted on chrome-plated Magnum 500 wheels.

Optional wheels included wire wheel cover, sports wheel cover, styled steel wheel, and a chrome Magnum 500 steel wheel. The traditional wire wheel cover was available as an option on all other models except Mach 1, Boss 302, and Boss 429.

Ford referred to the sports wheel cover as "luxurious," but it was actually sportier looking. This wheel was standard on the Mach 1 and available as an option on all other models, except those equipped with the 200-ci six-cylinder engine.

The styled steel wheel was a racing-style steel wheel with a wide chrome trim ring and five traditional air slots. This wheel was optional on all models except those with the 200-ci six-cylinder engine, Boss 302, or Boss 429.

The chrome Magnum 500 steel wheel was a traditional-looking steel wheel with five spokes and blacked out recessed areas between the spokes. It was only available on Boss 302 and Boss 429 models.

TOP: Identical to the 1969 model, heating and ventilation controls for 1970 were in the center of the instrument panel, down near the console. ABOVE: The optional air conditioning system for 1970 is shown here with the Decor Group. BELOW LEFT: The standard wheel cover was a hubcap and trim ring. *Fast* Eddie Stokes BELOW RIGHT: Magnum 500 wheels were standard on Boss 302 and Boss 429 models.

FAR LEFT: The styled steel wheel was optional on all models except the six-cylinder, Boss 302, and 429 models. *Tom Shaw*

LEFT: The sports wheel cover was standard on Mach 1. Even though it was just a wheel cover, it was perfectly suited to the car.

Shelby Mustangs

The final year for the Shelby Mustang was 1970. In actuality, the 1970 Shelby was a renumbered 1969 model. The only changes were the addition of a chin spoiler from the Boss 302 and two black stripes on the hood. The car's serial numbers were also revised. The "9" (indicating 1969) was changed to a "0" (indicating 1970). The rest of the car was identical to the previous model year.

Increasing insurance premiums and gas prices, along with the public's waning interest in muscle cars, spelled the end of an era. Carroll Shelby saw the writing on the wall and wisely decided to bow out from Shelby Mustang production. His legendary cars are incredibly valuable collector's items today and will live on forever in the hearts of performance car fans.

ABOVE: The 1970 Shelbys received the chin spoilers from the Boss 302. *Tom Shaw*

RIGHT: The 428 Cobra Jet pretty much filled the Mustang's cramped engine bay. *Tom Shaw*

This 1970 Shelby GT500 is parked on a lonely Colorado back road. *Joyce Davidson*

Appendix

Special Limited Production Mustangs

The 1968½ California Special Mustang: Custom Made for a Custom Market

It's amazing what a little clout can do. It's even more amazing what a lot of clout can do. This is the story of how one region of the country can carry enough weight to demand (and get) a customized car designed and built specifically to meet its needs. We're talking about Southern California's Ford dealers, and the hottest automotive market in the entire United States.

Back in 1967, with total annual sales hitting a staggering 472,121 units, Mustangs were still the hot ticket. Ford's little pony car was handily outselling all the other competition combined, although the new Camaro was certainly starting to take its share of the pie. And change was in the wind.

Although it was still the market leader in 1968 with sales at 317,404 units, Mustang sales were down approximately 25 to 30 percent. The early

part of the model year got off to a bad start for many reasons. A factory strike in the fall of 1967, along with increasing public interest in the Camaro sure didn't help. But what hurt Mustang sales the most, ironically, was in-house competition from Ford's own newly styled Torino and Mercury Cougar.

While most other car companies would be ecstatic to grab 317,000 sales, Ford was concerned and dubbed the Mustang market "very soft." The slumping numbers were felt especially hard in Southern California, where Mustang purchases made up a full 20 percent of the national sales totals. The Los Angeles area was always Ford's largest and most loyal market.

Southern California Ford Dealers, headed up by L.A. sales District Manager Lee S. Grey, got all fired up about this turn of events and decided to do something about it. Some creative marketing was in order, and Grey was one of Ford's best sales managers.

The vents on the hood of the 1968 High Country Special were non-functional but housed the turn signal indicators. *David Newhardt*

From 1966 to 1968, Colorado Ford dealer sold a High Country Package for Mustang. *David Newhardt*

The emblem on the nonfunctional scoop was indentical to the previous year, but the year was updated to 1968. *David Newhardt*

For 1968, many of the GT/CS elements were included on the high country special. *David Newhardt*

With the massive sales clout of the Southern California market behind him, Grey headed over to Shelby American's Los Angeles airport facility to see what he could do to put an end to the now officially declining Mustang market.

What Grey found was that Shelby had been working on a prototype Shelby notchback coupe. The car had been dubbed "Little Red" for its Ferrari Red paint hue. It was actually a concept vehicle that combined two ongoing projects: An experimental blown 428 cubic inch motor and an experimental customized decklid made out of fiberglass. It was essentially a hand-assembled project car and probably would have become a regular 1968 Shelby production if Grey hadn't shown up that day.

With the wheels in Grey's head spinning, he tried to envision this hot Shelby conversion being executed at the dealership level on 1968 Mustang notchbacks. But with custom side scoops and a totally different decklid/rear quarter treatment, Grey couldn't see any dealer being able to pull this one off. If this was going to be done, it had to be done right; factory style.

Grey decided to take his case (and Little Red) directly to Ford. He set up a meeting with then national car sales manager Lee Iaccoca. Grey was proposing a special "Southern California only" Mustang, and Iaccoca flipped over

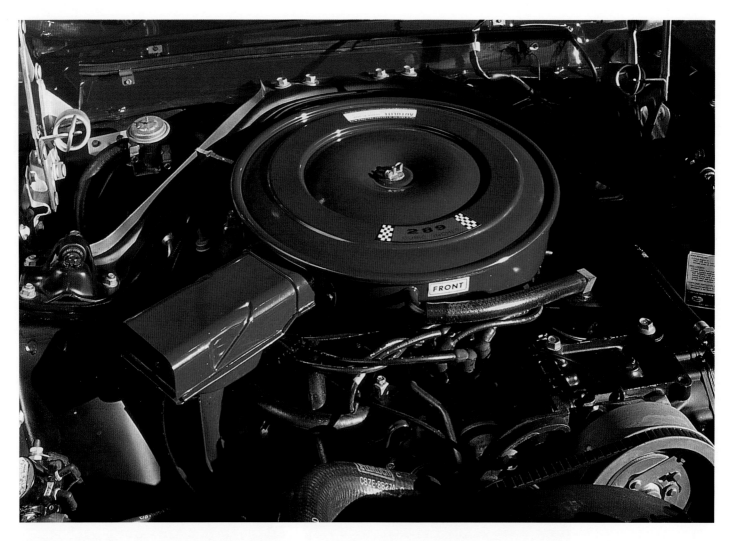

the idea. Little Red was then shipped to Ford's corporate headquarters in Dearborn for big brass scrutiny. The green light was given for Shelby to build a prototype variation of Little Red based on the Mustang GT's notchback-only platform, minus the blown 428. Sometime during the winter of 1967 and 1968, Ford rubber stamped full-time production of the California Special to be built exclusively at the San Jose plant. There was one stipulation that the car would first have to get the approval of Ford dealers in the rest of California. As they say, the rest is history.

Once the California Special Mustang was given approval, Shelby Automotive was contracted to produce special parts sets to be shipped by rail to Ford's San Jose production plant. Actual GT/CS (as the car was now referred to as) production began in late February of 1968, officially making the car a 1968½ model.

During its on-again/off-again production (the San Jose plant was closed temporarily due to base Mustang overproduction), a total of 4,325 California Special Mustangs were built. As orders from California dealers were satisfied, more GT/CSs were shipped to 13 western states and the British Columbia/Alberta area of western Canada. The last known GT/CS rolled out of the San Jose plant on July 18, 1968.

When you ordered a California Special, you had your choice of just about any engine and transmission combination. The base engine was the 200 cubic inch six with the 289 2 bbl. V-8 offered as the base V-8.

The 1968½ GT/CS may not have been an overwhelming success for Ford, but it did offer Californians a unique piece of Mustang history in the legendary Shelby tradition.

1967 Ski Country Special

Denver area Ford dealers created a promotional package available only on hardtops and fastbacks. Titled the Ski Country Special, these Mustangs were advertised in the Denver District in December 1967. The Mustangs were available in the following colors: Aspen Red, Vail Blue, Winter Park Turquoise, Loveland Green, and Breckenridge Yellow. This promotion was also available on the Galaxie, Fairlane, and Bronco in 1967.

Ski Country Special equipment included ski rack, coffee bar (luggage rack), limited slip axle, special emblems, window decals, and snow tires.

The 1968 High Country Special was available in any engine or color combination.
David Newhardt

The 1970 Twister Special was available in the Kansas City sales district. This car was built for people who wanted pure performance. *David Newhardt*

1967 High Country Special

Another Denver area special package, the 1967 High Country Special Mustangs once again appeared in the same colors that were offered in 1966: Timberline Green, Columbine Blue, and Aspen Gold. All came with special emblems that dealers could mount where they wanted. The 1967 High Country Special was available in all three body styles (hardtop, fastback, convertible)
.

1967 Stallion Mustang

The 1967 Stallion Mustang was a custom-designed car marketed and sold by Mainway Ford in Toronto, Canada. Only eight Stallions were ever produced. Four featured the 289 Hi-Po engine, and four received the big-block 390. A four-speed manual transmission or a C6 auto transmission could be ordered. The exterior of these cars were adorned with special paint, Stallion emblems, Cougar taillights, and a unique vinyl side tape treatment.

1967 Branded Special

The Branded Special was actually a kit distributed to Ford dealers near the end of the 1967 model year to help push pre-owned Mustangs on the used car lot. The kit featured a black floral pattern vinyl top with red or gold side stripes and emblems on the side of the roof. There was also a lasso with a horse running across it and the word

"Branded" above it. These items were to be added to the used Mustang and then the car was put on the lot with a specially discounted price. The emblems and vinyl roof kit have actual Ford part numbers.

1967 Blue Bonnet Special

The Dallas, Texas, area featured a Blue Bonnet Special Mustang. These were specially prepared hardtops only and were based on the 1967 Sports Sprint option. They were sprayed Blue Bonnet blue and came with a blue standard interior. Texas-shaped Lone Star Limited medallions and a running horse were placed on each fender.

1967 Sports Sprint

To fire up new car sales in the spring, Ford offered a special package for the Mustang called the Sports Sprint. Available on all three body styles, the package included a GT hood, full wheel covers, exterior appearance package, and a chrome air cleaner lid with a Sports Sprint insignia. Newly available colors were also offered for this spring special model.

1968 California Special—GT/SC

There were approximately 4,325 GT/CSs manufactured. Strangely enough, the promotion did not meet all of its sales goals, so the California Dealers got a little help from the Denver Sales District. The 1968 High Country Special was born.

1968 High Country Special

The 1968 High Country Special was pretty much a direct copy of the GT/CS project and differed only in that the GT/CS stripe on the side scoop received High Country badging. The general theory is that there were 251 High Country Special Mustangs built. Like the GT/CS, the HCS was available with any engine or color combination.

1968 Gold Nugget Special

The Gold Nugget Special is a unique Mustang that was sold out of the Seattle District Sales Office in 1968. There were 525 Sunlit Gold Mustangs built that featured special golden plaques on the dashboard engraved with the original owner's names. The cars also received a special louvered hood with black stripes. All Gold Nugget Special Mustangs were designated with the DSO 74 number (Seattle) plus the four digits 1111 and the color code Y (Sunlit Gold).

1968 Colors of the Month Mustangs (Denver Sales District only)

Here's a unique concept: paint color coding Mustangs to correspond with the individual month! During the first four months of the 1968 calendar year, Ford's Denver Sales District promoted

Half of the 96 Mach 1s with the 428 SCJ engine had C-6 Cruise-O-Matic transmissions, and the other half had four-speed manuals. *David Newhardt*

certain colors for each month, corresponding to the Holidays in each month. January brought about Black Hills Gold, February utilized Passionate Pink for Valentine's Day, March featured Emerald Green for St. Patrick's Day, and April's feature was Easter Time Coral. The Passionate Pink cars were known as Playboy Pink or Playmate Pink. Produced in extremely limited numbers, roughly 10 of these cars were built each month. The paint code on the trim tag of the Color of the Month cars was left blank.

1968 Cardinal Special

The Cardinal Special Mustang was made available in the Virginia/North Carolina area. Information on these cars is rare, but to the best of my knowledge the cars were painted either white or red and featured a red Cardinal sitting on a branch with the words "Cardinal Special" on the logo. This logo was positioned on the C-pillar. All Cardinal Specials were derived from the 1968 Sprint package and were available with both the six- and eight-cylinder engines.

1968 and 1969 Rainbow of Colors Mustangs

Rainbow Color Mustangs were sold in the Los Angeles and San Jose Districts (DSOs 71 and 72, respectively). California dealers touted this promo throughout 1968 and 1969. Rainbow Mustangs were offered in exciting hues such as Madagascar Orange, Whipped Cream, Caribbean Coral, Spanish Gold, Moss Green, Hot Pink, Forest Green, Sierra Blue, and Dandelion Yellow.

The initial order for the Mach 1s were to be all 428 Super Cobra Jets, but there weren't enough for all, so half recieved 351 Clevelands.
David Newhardt

The Twister Special name is fitting for Kansas City, which is famous for its extreme weather.
David Newhardt

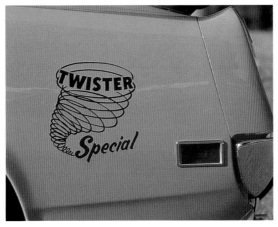

Limited Edition 600

The Limited Edition 600 was a promotion conceived and executed by the Philadelphia sales district (DSO 16) throughout May and June 1969. The 600 was a special order of custom colored Mustangs in Groovy Green or Flower Power Red. Available on hardtops or SportsRoofs, only 503 600s were ever produced. The Limited Edition 600 promotion was launched at the same time as Ford's national Mustang Stampede sales promotion. All 600s will be identified by the absence of a color code and a DSO of 16 plus a 2783 through 2788 number on the door data plate. Most 600s were powered by six-cylinder engines, with the largest available engine being the 351 2 barrel V-8

1970 Sidewinder Special

The 1970 Sidewinder Special is a 351 four-barrel–equipped SportsRoof Mustang that was sold in the Oklahoma City Sales District (DSO 65). The car was available in a wide variety of colors with a decal similar to Ford's own "snake on wheels" Cobra logo. The decal stripe kits came in a box in the trunk from the factory (only produced in Dearborn) to be applied by the dealers. It is believed that approximately 40 cars were Sidewinder Specials.

1970 Twister Special

The Twister Special was a specially prepped Mustang devised by the Kansas City Sales District (DSO 53). A total of 100 Mustang Mach 1s were ordered to be featured at the driveaway promotion called Total Performance Day. This promotion at the Kansas City International Raceway in November 1969 featured appearances by the Ford Drag Team, Ford's Total Performance Show, and Bob Tasca's High Performance Show. The gala event featured 96 Grabber Orange Mustang Mach 1s and 90 Calypso Coral Torino Super Cobra Jets emblazoned with special graphics featuring a large Twister on the quarter panel and a Shaker Scoop option. All cars were to be originally equipped with the 428 SCJ, but a shortage of big-block engines dictated that half the cars sport the new 351 Cleveland four-barrel engine.

Index